The Age Concern England Handbook

Second Edition

The publication of this Handbook which will, we are confident, be a valuable contribution towards the Age Concern movement was made possible by a generous grant from the National Westminster Bank PLC for which we are most grateful.

The Age Concern England Handbook
Second Edition
© Age Concern England, 1985
ISBN 0 86242 034 2
First Edition 1982
Published by Age Concern England
Printed by Eyre & Spottiswoode Limited
at Grosvenor Press Portsmouth
Designed by Tom Sawyer

Foreword

National Westminster Bank feels very strongly that it should support as wide a range of projects as possible, both nationally and locally, which will improve the quality of life within our community. Our support programme includes assistance to the arts, sport and a large variety of social needs.

We are, therefore, delighted to help Age Concern in the production of this Handbook which will prove of great assistance to all those organisations working with, or on behalf of, elderly people.

The Rt Hon the Lord Boardman MC TD DL
Chairman of National Westminster Bank

Introduction

This is the second edition of the Age Concern Handbook. It replaces the original booklet published in 1982. Many of the issues raised are the same. Some differ in emphasis, and others in substance as the social context in which we live and work itself changes; but the fundamental principles which underly the work of Age Concern are constant. They are based on the recognition that older people must describe for themselves their needs and must play an active part in seeking to meet them. Now that older people represent nearly ten million electors, they have the potential to become an effective force able to influence political decisions and the standards of care which are provided for them throughout the country.

Age Concern England is a *confederation* of more than a thousand autonomous local groups and some 77 national organisations which come together in order to create a coherent and an effective movement. Each of the constituent members is an independent agency free to pursue its own policies and to adopt its own priorities. Age Concern England provides the means through which the common ground can be identified and common objectives can be pursued by a combination of practical action and advocacy.

This Handbook, therefore, describes the ways in which Age Concern sets about the tasks and values which underly its work in providing direct services. It then sets out a broader strategy for the nation as a whole if it is to meet the growing challenge of a greying society.

As the first edition made clear, it would be impossible to promote all these desirable objectives at the same time. However, what the Handbook can do is to provide a framework in which priorities can be identified over a wide range of headings. These confirm once again the simple, but often overlooked, fact that the social well-being of older people depends upon a very wide range of factors from the planning of the environment to the practice of good medicine.

These priorities also reflect matters over which individual citizens have direct control as well as those which depend on legislation or investment from the public purse. They are as much about our attitudes towards the ageing process in others (as well as within ourselves) as they are about a compassionate but detached response to some of the obvious difficulties which many older people encounter through isolation, indifferent health, inadequate incomes, inappropriate services or lack of choice.

The original statements resulted from a gradual process of crystallisation based on nearly forty years experience since the National Old People's Welfare Council was first established. This revised, and now updated, set of policies also involved extensive discussion throughout the country, involving people who give service as well as older people themselves.

However, part of Age Concern's responsibility is to provide a reminder that ageing can also be regarded as one of the triumphs of modern society; that older people are a resource, and that one of our tasks is to find ways of reversing roles so that they can continue to be able to contribute as active members of their community. This positive view of ageing is likely to be a feature of our work during the next three years when Age Concern will look for ways of celebrating this extraordinary phenomenon of modern times.

Another emerging feature will be an increasing involvement in Age Concern's policy-making by direct representation of older people themselves. An increasing number of pensioner organisations have been welcomed into membership during the past few years and appropriate adjustments are being made to the Constitution in order to give them greater direct involvement through the creation of a Retirement Forum which will have direct access to the Executive Committee.

The changing structure of British society through increasing numbers of members of ethnic groups is also reflected in Age Concern's responses to the needs of older people. This was expressed in the following terms by a recent resolution of the Executive Committee: 'Our intention is to respond to the needs of elderly people from ethnic minorities in the most appropriate ways possible in relation to their differing cultural traditions in the belief that they have the right to the full range of services available to all citizens without regard to colour, culture or language'. Now steps will be taken to translate these ideas into practical terms.

Whilst the Handbook is produced by Age Concern England, the campaigning statements on pages 49–127 have been agreed in consultation with the national Age Concern groups in Scotland, Wales and Northern Ireland. Age Concern functions in this respect as a United Kingdom movement although, of course, there will sometimes be differing emphasis in relation to national or regional variations in conditions, customs and legislation to take into account.

Lastly, we should like to express our gratitude to the members of staff who drafted these policies, to the members of the Governing Body who debated and approved them and who will help to carry them out, as well as to the National Westminster Bank for once again contributing towards the cost of this unique publication.

Ann Spokes,
Chairman

David Hobman,
Director.

June 1985

How it all began
(History of Age Concern)

Although the name Age Concern has been in use since 1970, the organisation is over forty years old. The 1939–40 evacuation of people from cities uncovered the hardship and in many cases poverty that a million pensioners were enduring; and this disturbing situation led the National Council of Social Service to convene a conference to consider the welfare of elderly people. As a result a committee was formed with representatives from national voluntary organisations and three government departments 'to study the needs of old people and encourage and promote measures for their well-being'. By 1955 the committee had become known as the National Old People's Welfare Council.

As the movement grew, old people's welfare committees were formed throughout the country, covering regions, counties, county boroughs, districts and parishes. They were autonomous bodies, sometimes operating within the framework of a Council of Social Service or Rural Community Council, and sometimes quite independently. But the work of both the NOPWC and these smaller local organisations was directed towards the same aim – the welfare of retired and elderly people.

By 1970 the work of the NOPWC had developed to such an extent that it became independent from the National Council of Social Service and it marked its new identity the following year with the adoption of the cover name – Age Concern. Three years later this was extended to Age Concern England.

A similar process occurred in Northern Ireland, Scotland and Wales with the result that there are now four national Age Concern organisations each with their own local groups which almost without exception have adopted the name Age Concern.

The independent administrations of Northern Ireland, Scotland and Wales perform a similar role to Age Concern England's; and the officers of the four nations meet together on a regular basis to exchange views and develop a common policy. Thus, in structure the movement is federal.

As illustrated in the diagram on pages 14–15, Age Concern England is governed by a committee made up of representatives from the local groups and from other voluntary organisations and professional associations. Although Age Concern England acts as the national centre, the local groups are independent organisations with complete autonomy.

As a registered charity*, Age Concern England raises funds from trusts, commerce, industry and individual donors. In recognition of its work Age Concern England also receives a grant from the Department of Health and Social Security. More details of fund-raising activities appear on pages 17–18.

If you would like more information about any of the four national organisations, here are their addresses:

Age Concern England Bernard Sunley House, 60 Pitcairn Road, Mitcham, Surrey CR4 3LL (Tel: 01-640 5431).

Age Concern Scotland 33 Castle Street, Edinburgh EH2 3DN (Tel: 031 225 5000).

Age Concern Wales 1 Park Grove, Cardiff, South Glamorgan CF1 3BJ (Tel: 0222 371566 or 371821).

Age Concern Northern Ireland 128 Victoria Street, Belfast BT2 7BG (Tel: 0232 245729).

Registration number 261794

The Structure

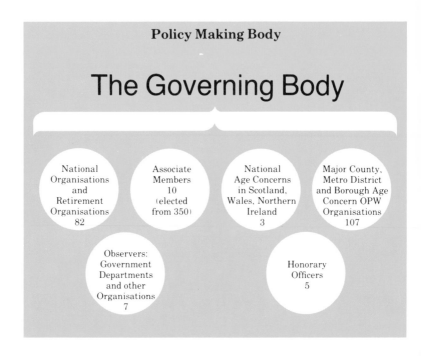

Policy Making Body

The Governing Body

National Organisations and Retirement Organisations 82	Associate Members 10 (elected from 350)	National Age Concerns in Scotland, Wales, Northern Ireland 3	Major County, Metro District and Borough Age Concern OPW Organisations 107

Observers: Government Departments and other Organisations 7

Honorary Officers 5

The Governing Body of the Society meets twice a year.
Every three years it elects the Honorary Officers and Executive Committee. The Executive Committee which meets quarterly appoints a Finance Committee, and Working Parties or Advisory Groups on special subjects as circumstances require.

Compiled January 1985

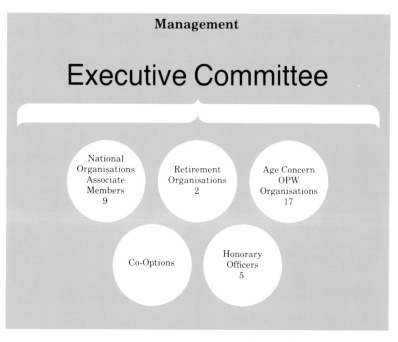

Management

Executive Committee

National Organisations Associate Members 9

Retirement Organisations 2

Age Concern OPW Organisations 17

Co-Options

Honorary Officers 5

Finance

Finance Committee

National Organisations Associate Members 1

Age Concern OPW Organisations 2

Co-Options

Honorary Officers 5

Services provided by Age Concern England

Administration and finance

Among the many services provided by Age Concern England's Administration and Finance Departments is the special insurance scheme. As a service for local committees and old people's clubs, insurance may be taken out at favourable premiums for public liability (third party) cover, personal accident cover for voluntary helpers and for loss of club money, and for employer's liability cover. Special cover is also available for loss of no claims bonus for voluntary drivers. For individual elderly people insurance is available for sickness on holidays, theft of money from gas and electricity meters, as well as household contents cover. The Finance Department also offers a bureau pay-roll service to Age Concern groups on a limited basis.

Fieldwork

The Fieldwork Department is the main contact and support point for the network of Age Concern groups throughout England. Working through a team of regionally-based Field Officers, the Department encourages good practice in services for elderly people, advises on a wide range of organisational matters and is responsible for the development of major Age Concern groups in areas where none exist.

Each Field Officer is responsible for working with a number of major Age Concern groups and each has a specialist interest in one important aspect of work, being available to advise colleagues in the Age Concern movement and other organisations.

The Department convenes regular regional meetings for the Chief Officers of major groups and for Chairmen. It administers the Annual Conference for staff working in the Age Concern movement. In addition to personal advice and support, Field Officers are responsible for the production of written material for reference by Age Concern groups.

A working party of representatives from groups throughout the country and Age Concern England staff has examined the needs of Chief Officers, Chairmen, Honorary Officers and other staff now running their organisations in rapidly changing social, political and economic environments. Its report outlines an action programme which is being actively pursued throughout the country. It includes induction, staff development, training, mutual support and the development of management skills.

Field Officers are concerned with helping groups to manage projects which are financed, often on a short-term basis, by central and local government agencies and health authorities. In particular, the Department administers funds under the Government's *Opportunities for Volunteering* and *Helping the Community to Care* programmes as well as Age Concern England's own Operation Enterprise, Development and Loan Funds.

In addition to continuing advice, the Fieldwork Department concentrates on helping Age Concern groups at times of crisis or transition. In particular, Field Officers work with review groups and encourage all Age Concern organisations to examine their operations and services regularly in the light of the needs of elderly people. The Department provides an essential communications link between people and organisations throughout the country and with Age Concern England.

Personnel

A small Personnel Department provides a service to Age Concern England and in conjunction with the Fieldwork Department offers an advisory service on employment matters to Age Concern groups. Advice on labour law, employee relations, and terms and conditions of employment are included.

Fundraising

It would be impossible for Age Concern England to provide its field and central support services for Age Concern groups, and for retired and elderly people generally, without relying heavily on the support received from voluntary donations, covenants and legacies. The Fundraising Department has the responsibility of raising these funds from commerce and industry, private donors, charitable trusts and foundations.

The Department also seeks sponsorship for many of Age Concern England's own projects.

Revenue obtained by the Department is also allocated to the Operation Enterprise Fund which makes grants to community projects run for the benefit of elderly people by local organisations. These grants are often the key element in getting a new service started in conjunction with local expertise and funding from other sources.

The Development Fund, which assists the establishment of new Age Concern groups in the initial phases of their existence, also benefits from the revenue raised by the Fundraising Department. In addition, voluntary donations support the small 'Urgent Needs' Fund, and also 'Lifeskills', a project which encourages older people to use their talents to help others.

The Department is always ready to assist local Age Concern groups in their own fundraising efforts by answering queries, periodically issuing guidance notes and other advice and by personal visits to consult with the officers or committee members of groups on their fundraising plans and problems.

Information

At a national level, information is co-ordinated through the Information Department which operates a comprehensive service for Age Concern groups and for any organisations working with elderly people. Information gathering extends to a series of unique directories of local action in a number of fields as well as to information retrieval exercises monitoring the effect of statutory initiatives and changes in public policy.

The Information Department deals with over 16,000 enquiries annually, offering information and advice to elderly people, their carers, Age Concern groups, Government Departments, local authorities, housing associations, private companies, journalists and researchers.

The Information Officers, who each specialise in one area of work, prepare policy briefings and responses to consultative documents from the Government and other organisations. The Officers work closely with the Parliamentary Officer and Public Relations Department in developing campaign issues and monitoring legislation.

The Department's monthly *Information Circular* commands a wide readership both within and outside the Age Concern movement, keeping its readers up to date on the latest developments affecting elderly people. Factsheets are produced which cover the most common problems affecting retired people on subjects such as heating, housing and making a Will and each year *Your Rights* is revised by one of the Information Officers.

Marketing

The Marketing Department is responsible for the sale and distribution of Age Concern England publications, including fundraising and promotional material. Through *Marketing News*, which is sent to Age Concern groups every two weeks, the Department provides information on publications, merchandise of special interest to elderly people, and suggestions to groups on marketing such items at a local level.

Through special mailings the Department aims to increase the distribution of publications to Area Health Authorities, Social Services Departments, hospitals, residential homes and other organisations involved with the welfare of elderly people. The sale of the two most popular publications – *Your Rights for Pensioners* and *Your Taxes and Savings in Retirement* – to a number of major national employers as part of their pre-retirement plans, is a successful example of such marketing initiatives.

The Department also sells publications at conferences and exhibitions.

The overseas market is developing rapidly as more countries experience the ageing of their populations and the Department is extending its sales initiatives in the international field. The workshop at Mitcham within Bernard Sunley House is another responsibility of the Department, and is attended regularly by local elderly people.

Parliamentary Liaison

Age Concern England's Parliamentary Office forms a direct link between MPs and members of the House of Lords and the Age Concern movement, both nationally and locally.

Secondly, the Parliamentary Officer acts as Research Assistant to the All Party Parliamentary Group for Pensioners in the House of Commons, arranging meetings with the many different organisations representing elderly people's interests such as Pensioners' Voice and the British Trades Union Action Association, and bodies, such as the BBC and the fuel boards, whose policies directly affect pensioners. The Parliamentary Officer carries forward the work which is generated out of these meetings, including the preparation of representations to Government Ministers, Parliamentary Questions, and the issuing of press releases.

The Parliamentary Officer briefs MPs and Peers about debates and legislation and their likely implications for elderly people and briefs Age Concern groups on matters they might wish to take up locally or nationally. The Office also organises Age Concern's meetings at each of the party political conferences.

Examples of issues on which the Parliamentary Office has been particularly active include the Housing Benefit Bill, alterations in charging procedures for residential accommodation and successive proposals about pensions. Another major task has been to develop a response to the Government's Social Services Review.

Every year, the Parliamentary Officer is involved in the preparation of a pre-Budget letter to the Chancellor of the Exchequer, setting out Age Concern's view of what pensioners need from the Budget, and responding to the Budget statement when it is released.

Public Relations

The Public Relations Department promotes the work and views of the Age Concern movement as a whole as well as Age Concern England's national activities such as conferences, training courses and publications.

Examples of recent campaigns co-ordinated by the Department include *We Care with a Chair, Help Age Concern Warm up Winter, Get Together with Age Concern* and *Accident* together with the Royal Society for the Prevention of Accidents. Future plans include a joint campaign with the Health Education Council: combining with animal welfare charities for a campaign on pets and elderly people; work on sensory loss; and a campaign demonstrating elderly people's contribution to society.

The Department has produced a video *Age Concern in Action*, an exhibition, and many leaflets, stickers and posters for use by local Age Concern groups. Speakers are provided for major events around the country.

Press releases and articles from the Press Office draw the media's attention to Age Concern projects of national interest. On request the Press Office can occasionally organise publicity for local Age Concern meetings and reports. Help is also given to journalists researching relevant issues, and Age Concern media coverage is monitored.

The Press Office produces annual lists of local programmes and newspaper columns on older people's interests and of national programmes which often feature Age Concern material. This helps Age Concern groups publicise their work more effectively. Further back-up material on the media is also prepared by the Press Office for the *Information Circular*.

Publishing

Publications provide a means through which Age Concern England can describe its policies, provide information, encourage new service initiatives, stimulate informed discussion, disseminate research and support training. Publications are designed for use by elderly people themselves, by those who work with them and by social scientists and people working in Government Departments. A selection of titles appears on page 132.

The Publishing Department produces around twelve titles a year, and is constantly exploring new ideas and looking for new authors. Two of its publications, *Your Rights* and *Your Taxes and Savings*, are updated annually. The Department welcomes the opportunity to consider ideas for articles and booklets from people working both inside and outside the Age Concern movement.

Recent new titles for elderly people include *Gardening in Retirement* and *Heating Help in Retirement. Old Age Abuse* designed for professional carers by Mervyn Eastman aroused a great deal of interest when first published in June 1984, while forthcoming publications include a book on the distressing problem of mental illness in old age; a guide to medicines and remedies and a book for widows. Meanwhile, the Department continues to produce the journal *New Age* and the bulletin *Age Concern News* on a quarterly basis. The Department has its own in-house print facility.

Research Unit

The development of new initiatives and the improvement of services for elderly people require a process of monitoring and evaluation. Knowledge is essential in campaigning for more resources and highlighting deficiencies in existing provision.

The Research Unit has been reviewing various examples of local provision: a psychogeriatric service; an intensive domiciliary support scheme; family placement/fostering schemes; chiropody services as well as alternative approaches to day care. A major study of ethnic minority elderly people has recently been completed, *Black and Asian old People in Britain* 1984.

At a local level, several pieces of the Unit's work are having an impact on policies, particularly for ethnic minorities, the mentally-frail and the consumers of meals on wheels and home care services.

The major staff and resource investment is currently focused on action research. The home support projects being carried out in collaboration with the Department of Psychiatry at Guys Hospital Medical School aim to assess the limits of care in the community, to determine the cost and to profile those elderly people who are sustainable at home. These projects are providing intensive but flexible 'packages' of domiciliary support to seriously mentally-frail old people, employing paid carers and co-ordinating other services in an endeavour to make services fit the unique needs of the 'clients'.

Another area of action research is providing foot health care, information and advice including shoe fitting at home as well as in clubs and centres. The aim is to assess the effect such a service would have on mobility, the capacity for self-care as well as the potential impact on other services, such as home help and residential care.

As pressure on public budgets increases and as Age Concern groups try to apply a needs-based approach, there is an increasing number of requests from service providers for statistical information not readily available from any other source. Resources are now being sought to offer a data base analysis service based on the needs, profile and future population distribution of various groups of older people.

The Unit has been able to respond to a range of questions raised by MPs and councillors. Studies on drugs and screening have also been completed and a study of shopping expectations and experiences among older consumers is being carried out.

Money for most of the Unit's research programme has to be raised for each individual project. Thanks go to the many foundations, trusts, research councils, central and local government departments who have funded this work to date.

The Unit continues its research findings through the *Research Perspectives of Ageing* series and is constantly looking for new ways in which to contribute to an understanding of ageing and old age, or to any area of policy or practice affecting older people. To this end, the Research Unit collaborates closely with a wide range of other agencies, including local Age Concern groups, to evaluate new initiatives and develop appropriate services.

Training

Age Concern England's Training Department runs over 60 courses a year on a wide variety of subjects. It also produces training material for use by other trainers from other agencies.

The Department is in a position to help local trainers throughout the country in planning courses for both voluntary and professional workers, and to advise staff of colleges and universities on suitable material for use with students.

The Training Department also offers advice on new developments in the care of elderly people in conjunction with the Information Department to broaden the scope of training and staff development.

A substantial bank of in-house training materials, together with advice on books and films can be made available on request.

Since September 1982 the Department has held its courses at Age Concern's national Training Resource Centre, Seebohm House, in Birmingham, the lease for which was purchased through a generous grant from the Department of Health and Social Security (DHSS).

Innovative Services

Age Concern continues to explore new ways of meeting the needs of old people, and in recent years has been responsible for initiating a number of projects which have sparked off interest both within and beyond the Age Concern movement.

Elderly People as Consumers

A working party with a membership representing a wide cross section of High Street traders and general consumer interests has been meeting to produce a report showing how the needs of elderly shoppers could be better met. Although the majority of individual old people have very little to spend in the market place; together they represent a very large sector of the consumer market place and it is in their interest, as well as shopkeepers, to pay greater attention to their needs where they differ from more active and affluent members of society. A generous grant from the Sainsbury Trust has made it possible to conduct an extensive survey.

Law and Vulnerable Elderly People

A consultative document will be produced on this important subject with detailed proposals for consideration following an extensive study by a group of experts on law and public administration. Among topics treated in the report are the management of financial affairs, consent and legal representation. Comparisons will be drawn between the protection and safeguards built in to the law relating to children and vulnerable adults, together with consideration of the statutory duties placed on public bodies for the welfare of old people.

Funeral Planning Societies

The National Steering Group to promote Funeral Planning Societies was established in January 1983 under the chairmanship of the Director. Its founding members include representatives of religious organisations, pensioner bodies and major national voluntary organisations. Its aim is to encourage the establishment of local Societies to alleviate the worries which many elderly people face as they approach death about their funeral arrangements and also to try to reduce the costs to the individual. The first local Society which was set up in the Salford area in January 1984 already appears to be meeting a need. It is expected that other Societies will form throughout the country.

Housing

The reports of two Working Parties were published in the autumn of 1984. *Sheltered Housing for Older People* examined the role of sheltered housing within the spectrum of care and accommodation needed by elderly people, one of its main conclusions being that sheltered housing should be regarded as essentially housing rather than as part of care provision. The Working Party expressed the hope that the Government would encourage local authorities to spread some of the benefits of sheltered housing, such as warden services and alarm systems, to elderly people in their own homes.

Housing for Ethnic Elders, the report of a joint Age Concern/Help the Aged Housing Trust Working Party, examined housing and related problems. A principal recommendation was that consideration must be given to making separate provision for older people from minority groups, when this is requested. One of the main hopes expressed for the future is that providers of housing will employ staff from ethnic minority groups in order to foster better relationships with the local ethnic community.

Counselling

Following the experimental bereavement counselling schemes set up by Age Concern England with help from the DHSS, a national registration and accreditation system has been introduced. Local groups involved in such work are invited to apply to Age Concern England for details.

Certificates and window stickers are available for local schemes which meet the necessary standards of training and support for volunteer counsellors.

FREE

Education for people in later life is also a subject for Age Concern's attention. In 1981 this interest became a reality with the establishment of FREE (The Forum on the Rights of Elderly People to Education) based at Bernard Sunley House, Mitcham.

The Forum, which is supported by individuals and organisations representing a wide range of statutory and voluntary interests, seeks to promote educational opportunities for older adults through an exchange of information. It publishes a quarterly *Information Bulletin* and organises occasional conferences to focus on pertinent issues. It also seeks to inform the public, press and all levels of government about areas of concern.

Religious Organisations

The report of the working party on the role of religious organisations in the care and welfare of elderly people *Claim to be*

Heard called for greater involvement of churches and synagogues. As a result, the Christian Council on Ageing has now been formed as an independent organisation. The Secretary welcomes enquiries for opportunities to speak about its work. His address is: 15 Florence Road, Sanderstead, South Croydon, CR2 0PQ.

SAGA conciliation

By arrangement with SAGA Holidays PLC, Age Concern England provides an independent conciliation service for holidaymakers who have been unable to obtain an initial settlement of any complaint. A full-time conciliator and assistant offer a free service to help such complainants to reach an amicable solution. The service has now dealt with over two thousand cases.

Dignity in Death Alliance

This Alliance formed in 1978, of more than forty pensioners' organisations, voluntary bodies and churches, continues to press for an increase in the National Insurance Death Grant. The secretariat is currently provided by Age Concern England and the chairmanship is jointly held between the Director of Age Concern England and the Chairmen of the All Party Parliamentary Group for Pensioners.

International Links

Although Age Concern's work stems from the needs of older people in this country, the organisation has continued to play an active part in responding to enquiries from many parts of the world, in receiving overseas visitors, and in engaging with organisations which promote the exchange of information and useful international policy initiatives.

International Federation on Ageing

The IFA currently has its world headquarters at the offices of Age Concern England. The Director and Deputy Director of Age Concern England are, respectively, President and Secretary General of the IFA. It has official status with United Nations, the World Health Organisation, UNESCO and other international agencies. The IFA continues to act primarily as an information network and a forum for the discussion of policy ideas, but since the success of the United Nations World Assembly on Aging in 1982, it has established a modest skills exchange project to enable it to bring Third World practitioners and experts from some of the developed countries together for training in the provision of services for elderly people.

Eurolink-Age

A lobby was formed by Age Concern England in July 1981 on behalf of elderly people in Europe – Eurolink-Age. Membership of the group is open to pensioners' organisations, agencies working with elderly people and individuals who work on their behalf. Eurolink-Age has now established good contacts in all the EEC member states and played an active part in establishing an Inter-Party Group in the European Parliament.

Eurolink-Age enables its members to relate to the European Commission and Parliament. Through a regular newsletter, it communicates information and ideas and co-ordinates combined lobbying where this is appropriate. Eurolink-Age has also been funded by the European Commission to convene a number of seminars on subjects varying from mental health and housing to training for later life, and short-term family placement schemes. It was also heavily involved in the consultations leading to approval for a second anti-poverty programme which has, this time, identified elderly people as a priority client group.

The group has its offices with Age Concern England, and its contact address in Brussels is at Rue Père de Deken 39, 1040 Brussels.

Services provided by local Age Concern groups

As a symbol of community involvement with the needs, aspirations and problems of elderly people, local Age Concern groups provide a range of services for elderly people in their areas. These include information services, good neighbour schemes and organised holidays for the infirm. Many groups also operate transport schemes which enable housebound people to attend day centres and lunch clubs, which are themselves often run by Age Concern groups. In some areas Age Concern offers practical help, using volunteers to decorate elderly people's houses or tend their gardens. Most groups provide a visiting service for the lonely and the disabled and some operate a meals on wheels service. An example of recently developed service provided by some Age Concern groups is a hospital after-care scheme through which volunteers help elderly people cope with the difficult transition from hospital to home. The 'Priorities for Action' outlined on pages 33–40 of this Handbook identify the areas of most pressing need in the 1980s and suggest the services required to meet them.

The increasing number of very elderly people in the UK will inevitably require more community support. In a situation where statutory bodies are either unable or unwilling to meet the growing demand on services, more back-up support will have to come from the community – from families, neighbourhoods and local Age Concern groups.

*The booklet **Age Concern at Work** (also published by Age Concern England) describes in more detail the variety of services provided by local groups.*

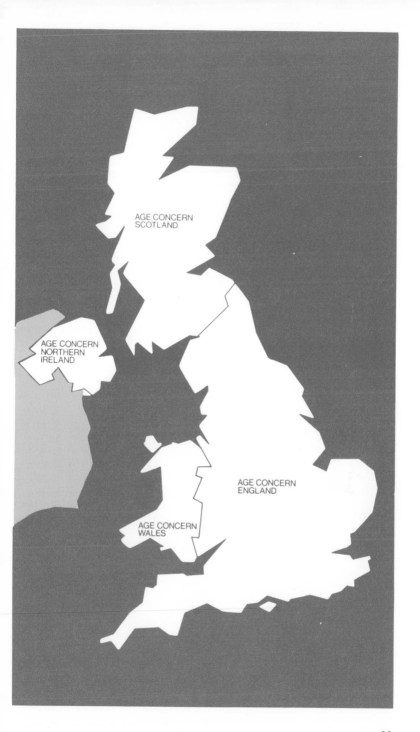

AGE CONCERN
SCOTLAND

AGE CONCERN
NORTHERN
IRELAND

AGE CONCERN
ENGLAND

AGE CONCERN
WALES

Fieldwork Priorities

CHALLENGE, OPPORTUNITY AND PARTNERSHIP

Challenge

Ageing presents one of the major social challenges for the remainder of the twentieth century. It is a challenge which can only be met by the co-operation of all involved, including elderly people themselves, their families, neighbours and friends, voluntary groups and statutory organisations. The Age Concern movement sees its task as presenting the scale and detail of the challenge and in mobilising resources to meet it.

Many elderly people, particularly those in their late 70 and 80s, will need some support in carrying out their tasks of everyday life; and some will require considerable support. Over the next 20 years, there will be a substantial proportion of the population over 60 and the proportion over 75 will grow at an even faster rate than before.

In 1976, one person in five was over 60, of whom one in four was over 75, and one in twenty-one over 85. By 1996 although the proportion over 60 will be about the same, one in three will be over 75 and one in thirteen over 85. The number of over 85s will have increased by 57 per cent over the 1976 figure. This trend is international: it is estimated that one-third of those people who have reached the age of 65 in the last 2,000 years are alive today!

The Age Concern movement is looking to play its part, jointly with others, in the process of identifying and meeting the challenges of the times. There is a clear need for an increased commitment on the part of all the groups who are concerned.

There is no doubt that statutory bodies will be unable fully to meet the demands which will be made upon them. Although they will continue to have major responsibilities which they cannot give up, more responsibility is also falling on voluntary bodies, including Age Concern, and even more on the community – families, friends and neighbours. The trend towards early retirement, be it voluntary or enforced, is creating additional stress now and may be a further complicating factor for the future. Co-operation and mutual support will be necessary to meet the challenge.

Opportunity

Elderly people should never become simply the recipients or the 'victims' of organised social care. Our purpose therefore is to meet the infinite variety of needs with an infinite flexibility of approach and a continuing sensitivity to the individual rights and integrity of each elderly person. Ageing is about opportunity as well as need, about the rights of elderly people as well as the responsibilities of others, and about self-help as well as outside support.

Old people are not a separate section of society: they are simply people who have grown older. Not all want or need the same things for themselves. Their needs and talents are as varied as those to be found in any other generation and they display the full range of human characteristics. What they should all have is the freedom to choose their life-style, to have their views heard, to command respect and to be able to influence events. At present these reasonable aspirations are denied to many elderly people through circumstances over which they have little or no control.

Many elderly people themselves need to be convinced of their value and usefulness and not influenced by too low an estimation of their comparative worth and significance. By the realisation of their rights and responsibilities as participating members of society, and by re-charging their own powers of self-reliance and self-help, they will be better equipped to assert their own claims to equal consideration. They will also be able to make an important, mature contribution to their society.

Partnership

Partnership between individuals and organisations and between organisations themselves will play an important part in meeting the challenges and opportunities of the times. Age Concern seeks to work co-operatively with many other groups. Firstly, we work in partnership with elderly people and those around them. Secondly, we co-operate at all levels with the caring services of local and central government. We seek the co-operation of policy-makers, planners and service providers throughout the services. We work with and influence politicians and senior officers: at the same time, we aim to work more closely with home helps, with general practitioners and with others at grass roots level.

Thirdly, we work with and influence other statutory authorities which affect the lives of elderly people. Housing Departments, leisure services, planning and transport issues are all areas of focus for the Age Concern movement. We also seek to promote co-operation between statutory organisations in the service of elderly people.

Fourthly, we work closely with other voluntary organisations and community groups in identifying and meeting needs. Age Concern may be able to help by providing services and support to other agencies.

At every level of Age Concern, we can play an important role in bringing groups together, in planning, in stimulating others to act, in co-operative work and in accepting the responsibility for our own action. We do not seek a leading role in this partnership, although sometimes it will be appropriate for Age Concern to take the initiative in bringing people together. Our aim is to participate as full partners in meeting challenges and accepting opportunities.

PRIORITIES FOR ACTION

The role of Age Concern

Discussions throughout the Age Concern movement and with our partners in other organisations have identified four basic functions for any Age Concern group:

1 Direct Intervention, including the provision of services, aims to help elderly people in need. This includes the organisation of direct help for those frail elderly people who need support, the encouragement of self-care and mutual aid, and preventive work. Our aim is to provide a full spectrum of support rather than simply to organise crisis support for those currently most in need. The mobilisation of volunteers is an important element in our approach, as is the provision of more support for informal care by relatives, friends and the community generally.

2 Social Advocacy involves public education and campaigning on behalf of elderly people, transmitting their views and needs to policy makers and the public at large. Our purposes are to influence legislation and decisions on specific issues, to encourage sensitive and caring attitudes amongst those who work with elderly people and to stimulate greater understanding and commitment in the wider community.

3 Innovation and Research is a function which reflects Age Concern's involvement in identifying and pioneering new projects, looking always for new ways of meeting needs and problems. We are committted to the principle of useful research, identifying new needs and opportunities, and monitoring existing work.

4 Partnership in Joint Social Planning involves a co-operative approach to identifying and meeting needs. It requires an openness and a willingness to participate as equals in planning and in working together. We work with voluntary and with statutory organisations, and with both together. We need to foster, within our own movement and outside, a capacity to respond to individual needs regardless of organisational boundaries and to encourage joint action and joint decision making on priorities. This co-operative approach includes campaigning and advocacy as well as direct service provision and sometimes involves alliances with other groups to represent the needs and problems elderly people face.

The Age Concern style

In pursuing these objectives, the Age Concern movement has developed a style which has three main components:
Firstly, our style is *responsive:* it is based on listening to what elderly people themselves say about their needs and aspirations. It is *participative*, involving them in creating and controlling their own solutions.

Secondly, it is *flexible* in its response: our starting point is always an individual with a unique personality and range of needs. We must not tailor individuals to meet our available services.

Thirdly, our structure is based on *local autonomy and independence*. Local groups identify priorities in their own communities and devise strategies to meet them. They have a capacity to unlock resources and match them to local needs.

The needs based approach

Our work must always take the needs of elderly people as its starting point. We can then work with elderly people to discover and implement solutions. There are many ways of working – some examples are campaigning for improved provision, the organisation of a specific voluntary service, and the encouragement of community support. The choice of a particular strategy is a practical one based on the assessment of need and the knowledge of local resources. An integral part of our work is a regular re-assessment of need and a constant monitoring of strategies.

The needs identified in this way provide the framework within which we can work to change attitudes and prepare younger people and the recently retired to help others and, eventually, themselves. Working across the spectrum of support, identifying and meeting needs at different levels, should give us the knowledge to intervene earlier to prevent or delay extreme needs. Prevention is becoming an increasingly important part of our overall approach.

The needs of old people

As a result of our work, Age Concern recognises many of the major needs of retired and elderly people in our society. We readily acknowledge that priorities vary from one area or one group to another, but we feel that it is useful to summarise them here. We are also aware that problems will be particularly acute in those areas including the inner cities and areas of retirement immigration which have a high proportion of elderly people in the population. Such categories are necessarily arbitrary. In broad terms, we are concerned with old age in society: in everyday life and separate needs listed here merge into each other. Our aim, having shown the areas of need, is then to stimulate flexible responses to individual cases. Our experience suggests that the major needs are:

1 Choice

In our society, ageing is often accompanied by a lessening of control by the individual elderly person over his or her own life and the forces which affect it. Some of the constraints are unavoidable: many are imposed unnecessarily and form a real restriction on the power of choice. Age Concern seeks to retain choice for elderly people to the maximum degree possible. This may involve widening the range of facilities available, providing elderly people with the cash to buy choice and the information on which to found it, or simply deciding to offer choices as an integral part of programmes of care. One important example is the promotion of the full range of choices appropriate to our multi-racial society.

Two important factors in enabling choice are *money* and *information and advice*. In a civilised society, every elderly person should be able to expect an adequate income guaranteed by the state. Such income is often the crucial factor in maintaining social relationships and mobility, in achieving and maintaining an adequate standard of accommodation, and in opening up a choice of life-style.

The Age Concern movement helps elderly people to claim their rights by providing welfare rights information and by publishing and distributing *Your Rights* and *Your Taxes and Savings in Retirement*. Throughout the country, Age Concern groups are responding daily to requests for advice.

Information and sensitive advice is often the key to choice. Age Concern groups are providing advice and information in many ways, including the publication of local information directories, the promotion of educational opportunities, the organisation of victims support schemes and the establishment of counselling schemes for those who have suffered loss. Many of these services are run in close collaboration with statutory services and with other voluntary organisations. Information about self-care is important and increasingly needed as care resources are stretched.

2 Health

Positive steps to maintain good physical and mental health are becoming an increasingly important facet of the work of the Age Concern movement. We are also concerned to find ways to help elderly people to cope with implications of disability, providing practical help and support to enable them to participate fully in society.

Examples of our work include the promotion of self-care, hospital after-care schemes, advice on exercise and nutrition, widespread day care services, stroke clubs, equipment loan services, hearing aid checks, and the provision of chiropody services.

Age Concern is also making an increasingly important contribution in the promotion and maintenance of mental health and in caring for the mentally frail. One example is the provision of practical and emotional support at times of crisis, a very relevant factor in recovery. Day care, all-round assessment and support, day and night sitting services, and support for caring relatives are all services which may be offered by Age Concern groups.

Support for those who care for elderly people in the community must be a high priority for all the caring services. The responsibility of care can be onerous and demanding: timely support can profoundly affect both the quality of such care and its duration.

It can easily be seen that the promotion of good health is an integral part of many community services. We are not concerned only with helping those in ill-health; education, information and activity are just as important in our overall approach.

3 Social Relations

Satisfying personal relationships are as important for elderly people as for other members of the community. The relationship between individual elderly people and the other people with whom they come into contact are a very important part of their lives. Age Concern promotes good social relations in a number of important areas.

Like everyone else, elderly people require *respect* and the opportunity to contribute something to society – time, skill, experience or wisdom. These are issues for public education and for campaigning – for many people, status is bound up with income and work, both of which can be denied to old people. Age Concern should use the skills of elderly people in meeting some of the problems of society, in encouraging retirement pensioners to help others, and in helping elderly people to participate in decision-making. In particular, we should work to encourage contact and mutual help across the generations.

A variety of schemes for *care and support* combat both isolation and loneliness. Street warden and good neighbour schemes are just two examples. Good visiting schemes can provide friendship and offer a means to discover and meet other needs. There is no reason, however, why our encouragement of social contact should stop at formally organised care schemes. Clubs and holidays are more important for many people. Our purpose here is to use our and their skills and knowledge to help elderly people do what they want to do in the company they choose.

Contacts with *family and friends* are the most needed and the most fulfilling social relationships. Age Concern seeks to foster and facilitate meetings and relationships based on affection and mutual interest. We also aim to blur the distinction between help based on friendship and formal 'care'. Community support may involve, amongst many other activities, encouraging self-help groups, providing sitting services and short-stay accommodation to relieve caring relatives. It also involves training professionals to search out and use the resources of neighbours, friends and volunteers. Age Concern seeks to maximise the use of community resources, campaigning for better training for professionals and greater public awareness of needs and opportunities.

4 Environment

The physical environment in which elderly people live indicates another range of needs. Here, we identify four major areas: accommodation, mobility, amenities and security.

In the first area the need is for *appropriate accommodation*, which may involve the provision of alternative accommodation, including short-term housing. Advice and information on housing issues is provided locally and nationally. Our campaigning role is also important. Issues on which Age Concern has campaigned include increased housing provision, support for elderly owner-occupiers, housing mobility, repairs and improvements, training for sheltered housing wardens and preventing the sale of local authority sheltered housing.

Age Concern helps by providing decorating, gardening and insulation schemes – services which can be an important element in maintaining social contact and providing a pleasant environment.

Mobility is one of the most important needs of elderly people. It is an area where the increasing number of elderly people and the continuing reduction in services are creating substantial problems. The answers include the provision of car and minibus transport for the disabled and house-bound, voluntary car services, aids and adaptations in the home, campaigning for rural bus services, and negotiating with transport undertakings for better facilities. At the most basic level of mobility, chiropody services are important.

Basic amenities should be available locally with good access for elderly people. Chemists' shops, post offices, corner shops, churches and many other facilities are important. Libraries and offices for all the regular payments which elderly people make should be sited close enough for ready use or brought out regularly to the customers.

Fear for their personal *security* and their property and in particular the fear of violent crime is a major part of many old people's lives. Age Concern aims to put the risk into proportion but has also worked and campaigned to minimise the risks, helping elderly people to protect themselves from violence, confidence tricksters and other forms of crime. Age Concern oversees a national system of identity cards for workers within our movement.

5 Leisure – activity and opportunity

Retirement is a time for leisure: there can be a wide range of opportunities for exciting, interesting, stimulating, fulfilling activity. Our purpose, once again, is to maximise those opportunities. Broadly defined, education can offer a host of possibilities. Formal or informal, organised or self-programmed, education can open up a wide range of knowledge and skills.

Many elderly people enjoy sport and recreation. Facilities for them could certainly be much more widely available. Craft skills can stimulate creativity and profit. Holidays can provide an interesting break. Age Concern also wants to extend the opportunities for elderly people as volunteers, giving and helping others in the community.

Of course, there is no reason why older people should be restricted to groups of elderly people in order to participate in these activities: their contribution can be through ordinary clubs and societies, through informal groups or even alone. A great deal remains to be done to integrate retired people fully into the range of opportunities for self-fulfillment. This principle does not only apply to younger, more mobile retired people. There are opportunities for older and disabled people as well.

Finally, it should be said that, although exercise and interest are of great importance, everyone has the right to choose to do nothing.

Meeting needs

There are many ways in which we can meet the variety of needs identified. These include the organisation of traditional services each defined by function; stimulating other organisations to meet the requirements; encouraging community-based approaches which aim to provide a flexible range of support for elderly people in need; the encouragement of self-care, self-help and mutal aid; collaborative provision, and campaigning for better services. In the Age Concern approach, each of these methods involves the direct participation of elderly people themselves in devising, modifying and providing their own contribution.

The essence of our approach is to work from a need to an appropriate solution or group of solutions. For instance, each of the approaches outlined above could be an appropriate way of dealing with a problem of mobility. We could organise a social car scheme, ask the postmistress to act as an informal clearing house for transport arrangements, stimulate car-sharing, set up a feeder system to regular bus routes in collaboration with the bus company, or campaign for revenue support for new bus services. Each of these strategies could be a valid way of meeting the need. Which strategy is chosen will depend on local resources and conditions.

Prevention

An emphasis on extreme needs does not present the whole of the picture. Many of the problems of older people are built in to their lives at an earlier stage. We aim to prevent and minimise problems by intervention and support for elderly people and carers before problems reach crisis point or before long-term care is required. We take a broad view of the needs of age, aiming to provide and stimulate a wide range of responses from all the available sources: statutory, voluntary, informal, self-help, and commercial. We also aim to inform younger generations about elderly people and to encourage preparation for growing old.

Each of the areas of need we have identified – choice, health, social relations, the environment, and leisure – can be met at crisis point for amelioration or, occasionally, cure. We can also work now to prevent problems arising or to minimise their impact. Education for retirement should start early in life. Retirement is most likely to be fulfilling if people can foresee problems and plan to avoid them. This increasing emphasis on prevention has implications for the work of all Age Concern groups. It also has implications for spending patterns and priorities in local and central government.

FOCUS ON THE FUTURE

Independence and co-operation

The Age Concern movement consists of Age Concern England, major Age Concern groups operating at the level of social service authorities, other established major groups, and local groups. It is usual for groups to be independent, separately registered charities with control over their own work and priorities. This autonomy has stimulated and encouraged the dynamic growth of the Age Concern movement: our emphasis is always on helping independent groups to assess and meet local needs, using their unique knowledge of local resources.

Experience suggests that, in principle, Age Concern groups should be independent of other local organisations – although independence of action should not lead to isolation nor preclude the sharing of common services where these are economic and practical. In some special cases, it is appropriate for groups to have formal or constitutional relationships with another body during a transitional period. In particular, we recognise the important role that many Community Councils and Councils for Voluntary Service have played in enabling Age Concern groups to establish the basis and resources for independent operation.

Whatever the individual local circumstances, every Age Concern group should have its own constitution or terms of reference: its policy making or executive committee should have full responsibility for the attraction and allocation of finances, the appointment of staff, the deployment of resources and the organisation of activities.

From this independent base, Age Concern groups work with other organisations in planning, in providing services, in joint programmes and in ad hoc alliances.

Funding

Age Concern groups receive financial support from many sources, including public funds. It is desirable not only to extend funding but also to diversify the sources of funds. We accept the necessary degree of accountability that is a condition of receiving and using public funds, but we believe that funding agencies should not seek to tie the hands of recipient organisations in a way that is inconsistent with the role of an autonomous voluntary organisation carrying out the full range of functions we have defined (see 'The role of Age Concern' pages 33–34).

At present, there is a move towards greater control by local authorities over voluntary groups which they support by grant-aid and, at the same time, increasing control by central government over local authority spending. There is also a substantial move towards the funding of projects rather than the general work of Age Concern organisations. Such projects aim to set up a specific service, such as a hospital discharge or good neighbour scheme, involve their own staff, and often have a finite life. Sponsorship of each project and the responsibility for management and for continuing the service after the life of the project remain with the Age Concern group. Age Concern groups should be able to maintain a core organisation which has the freedom to respond to a wide range of local needs and problems. Funding agencies should recognise the financial and workload implications of adding substantial management and project commitments to that core and accept their responsibility for support.

Age Concern groups are being asked to accept responsibility for a wide range of new services for which funding is available from statutory sources. Age Concern England will advise groups which face difficult judgements about priorities and the circumstances under which they should accept new responsibilities.

In our view, a major Age Concern organisation has a reasonable case for holding reserves equal to the cost of twelve months' operation. We strongly recommend funding agencies to recognise, as an absolute minimum, the rationality of holding six months' reserves and sufficient amounts to meet obligations including those to staff. These are necessary safeguards for the trustees of charitable organisations.

Financial planning and control, including proper budgeting and independently and professionally audited accounts, should be normal practice.

Support by Age Concern England

In general, Age Concern England will continue to direct its primary support services to major groups, whose boundaries are co-terminous with those of social service authorities. Such groups are registered charities and accept responsibility for the four basic functions of an Age Concern groups (see 'The role of Age Concern' pages 33–34). Normally, there is only one such group at the level of each local authority, but occasionally there may be several groups, each having a distinct complementary function or functions.

These support services include regular mailings to chief officers of major groups, the *Information Circular*, access to training information and courses, publications and the regular support of the field staff. Local groups have access to these services, but any intervention beyond the level of information provision will normally be done in consultation with major groups. Field staff may also be able to assist major groups in the development of local groups and services. Normally, Age Concern England's Field Officers serve as members of major group executive and management committees.

Age Concern England welcomes advice, information and comment from groups throughout the movement on issues which affect elderly people and on its own role and services. Communication may be direct to relevant Age Concern England staff, via Governing Body or Executive Committee representatives or through the medium of the Field Officer.

There are some areas where there are substantial Age Concern groups below the level of 'co-terminous' major groups. Support services are also provided to such 'non co-terminous' major groups where Age Concern England has considered it appropriate. Such major groups cover an identifiable and substantial area (such as a city, large town, non-metropolitan District Council area or distinct part of a Metropolitan District or London Borough). They provide a range of direct services to elderly people: usually employ staff; act as a communications link between local Age Concern groups in their area, and Age Concern England; and accept responsibility for the four basic functions.

Standards

Age Concern organisations need to be responsible, efficient and effective in the work they do; they also have a particular responsibility to be sensitive to those who support them, and those who use and man the services they provide.

The standards of work of every Age Concern organisation are of vital importance: firstly, because of the organisation's responsibility to elderly people and their families as well as to those who – as volunteers or otherwise – man the services; secondly, grant aid and public support cannot be attracted unless an organisation is seen to be effective and cost-effective; and, thirdly, a poor reputation will affect the credibility and willingness of people to approach it either to offer help or to ask for help.

Other sections of this document identify the areas of work in which standards are important – particularly in the identification and assessment of need and in the strategies we adopt to meet needs. Commitment to high standards also requires that groups should regularly review their activities, priorities, planning, and methods of operation. Every major group should formally do so in detail every three or five years. This will usually involve a working group, which may usefully bring in expertise and knowledge from outside the organisation, Age Concern England Field Officers will be pleased to service such groups or to provide advice and comments.

No Age Concern organisation should regard itself as having an inalienable right to exist. Its existence can only be justified by the relevance and effectiveness of its work. If any organisation is unable for any reason to provide the whole range of services needed in its area, its existence should not prevent the setting-up and support of other groups to carry out the necessary work.

Staffing and volunteers

Paid Staff

It is widely recognised that Age Concern organisations which maintain and deploy substantial resources and which need to extend and develop their work require the services of competent and experienced paid staff.

This fact imposes considerable responsibilities on management committees and professional chief officers who need to take decisions about the recruitment, training, deployment and support of staff.

It is important that these responsibilities are not ignored, or their relevance to the efficient running of the organisation minimised. In particular, chairmen and management committees need to ensure that proper systems of support and communication exist for and between staff, and should be alert to the changing responsibilities and roles of staff as the organisation itself evolves and develops. Age Concern England has provided guidance on these and related issues, including legal matters, in its *Management Handbook*.

We believe that key staff working in the Age Concern movement should be employed directly by the appropriate Age Concern organisation. Although joint appointments may be made in some circumstances or staff seconded from other agencies or authorities, safeguards should be built in to ensure an adequate role for Age Concern. In all such cases, the terms of such appointments and the responsibilities of each partner should be established clearly and in writing.

Officers and Committee Members

The individuals and representatives who make up the committees of Age Concern organisations, and the officers they elect, are key people within the Age Concern movement. The responsibility they bear requires that they should be seriously interested in their work as Age Concern officers. It is important that they should be prepared for this role, and that they should not feel inhibited about claiming reasonable expenses in attending meetings.

The Chairman is a key figure in any Age Concern organisation, being closely involved in supporting staff and formulating policies. Organisations will also have one or more Vice-Chairmen, who will share these responsibilities and who may deputise for the Chairman. The performance of the Chairman's role requires considerable commitment and this should be recognised in his tenure: it is advisable that a Chairman should not normally serve for more than three to five consecutive years at a time, which period will normally be specified in the Constitution.

The Treasurer has an important role in providing overall financial control and budgetary planning for his organisation, and in ensuring that proper accounts are kept and that a full audit is carried out annually. The Treasurer should not be given direct responsibility for fundraising, although one of his functions might be to ensure that suitable people are recruited to organise this work.

Volunteers

Volunteering is an integral and essential part of the Age Concern movement enabling people of all ages and with a wide range of experience and skills to offer to participate in its work.

The concept and nature of volunteering is developing and evolving in response to trends and local circumstances. As rising unemployment and changing patterns of work compel people to look for other ways of using their skills and time, voluntary work is acquiring a new significance and a wider appeal amongst people looking for new interests and new challenges. At the same time, an increasing emphasis on the value of 'community' based care for older people highlights the essential 'voluntary' contribution of friends and neighbours in the provision of this care. Thus Age Concern organisations have an important role in supporting and encouraging a very broad spectrum of voluntary activity, both within their organisation and in supporting the work of friends, neighbours and others caring for older people in the community.

While appreciating the scope and diversity of this activity, it is important that organisations are aware of their responsibilities in protecting the interests and rights of volunteers. While their work can bring a new and unique dimension to the activities of local groups, it is important that volunteers are never used simply as cheap labour or to replace paid staff.

People are attracted to voluntary work for many different reasons. They may be looking for an opportunity to meet new people, take up a new interest, become involved in an activity which they feel is valuable and worthwhile, or they may be looking for experience in order to improve their own employment prospects. It is important that organisations understand the motivation of their volunteers and try to meet their varied needs and expectations.

Volunteering should never be a static occupation. The needs and demands of volunteers will change, and they should be given every opportunity, with appropriate training and support, to develop their interests and talents as fully as possible.

As part of the Age Concern movement volunteers are involved in a wide range of activities – providing services, fundraising, campaigning and, as members of local Management Committees, assisting in the formulation of policy and the planning of new work. It is important that Age Concern groups are always alert to the possibilities of extending and developing the participation of volunteers within their agencies.

The careful selection of volunteers is crucial to the success of any volunteer project. Not all volunteers will be suitable and a careful and sensitive selection process is essential in order to protect the interests of the volunteer and the organisation.

Detailed job specifications for volunteers are important, both in clarifying the duties and time commitment involved, as well as in helping the organisation to think through the kind of training and support it should provide.

The provision of appropriate training for volunteers is a major responsibility in order to give them the knowledge, skill and confidence to do their work and also to maintain standards within the organisation. Training is also important as a way of creating a group identity amongst volunteers and increasing their commitment to the organisation and its work. It should be a continuous process which can be adapted to meet the changing needs and interests of the volunteers and may frequently involve a substantial input from professionals outside the agency.

In addition to formal training, continuing support and access to advice and help are also essential. Volunteers should have regular opportunities to review their work and to take on additional responsibilities or reduce their commitments as appropriate. It is also important that they should meet other volunteers in order to share their experiences and problems.

The successful integration of volunteers requires a commitment from the organisation as a whole and a clear understanding of the respective roles of all its members. Volunteers should understand the aims, structure and functions of the organisation and be fully briefed about their roles and responsibilities within it. They should be able to participate in its affairs and should be consulted on any decision affecting their work. It is particularly important that they feel that their contribution, however small, is recognised and appreciated.

Volunteers are not a cheap option. Every organisation should make sure that adequate financial provision is made to cover all out of pocket expenses incurred by volunteers as well as provision for training and support. Full insurance cover should also be provided for all volunteers.

Volunteers are the key resource within the Age Concern movement. It is essential that Age Concern organisation and their staff recognise the skills and commitment especially the time commitment required in their recruitment, selection, training and support.

The National Policy

The National Policy is intended as a guide within the Age Concern movement and for all those who seek to improve the quality of life of elderly people in our society. The areas covered are wide and many would need changes both in law and professional practice. Some are small measures capable of implementation in the short term; others require major alteration to our fiscal system. In some cases issues are put forward for consideration without a definite conclusion. They are important issues that require further research and understanding before the best way forward is clear.

Dilemmas abound: those who are old now must not be sacrificed for those yet to retire; seeking concessions for elderly people cannot be seen as a panacea. Above all Age Concern believes that elderly people should have sufficient income to choose their own way of life with wholehearted support from all the professionals involved in their wellbeing. There is a long way to go.

Policies introduced or substantially redrafted at the 1985 Age Concern England Governing Body Meeting are marked with an asterisk.

INCOME MAINTENANCE

Long Term View

1 An adequate level of income should be the right of all elderly people so that they can participate fully in the social and economic life of the community, exercising real choice in their patterns of expenditure.

2 A comprehensive and independent review of the present income maintenance system is required which should consider the structure, scope and interplay of income tax and other forms of taxation, national insurance benefits, non-contributory benefits, means tested benefits, and grants and concessions which contribute to income support. Any report should be subject to full public consultation.

3 Research is essential into the costs and potential effects of alternatives to the present system which will provide an integrated system sensitive to individual needs, intelligible to the general public and capable of removing the tax/benefit poverty trap. Alternative studies should include tax credit and negative income tax schemes, basic income guarantee and national minimum income schemes and universal allowances.

*4 Consideration should be given to whether retirement income and savings should be treated generously for taxation or benefit assessment purposes.

Short Term View

5 It is difficult to reconcile long term strategies with short term objectives, and the policies outlined are not all intended to provide an alternative solution to a co-ordinated long term re-appraisal which might require complete restructuring of pensions, Housing Benefit and Supplementary Benefit. They are put forward as temporary measures to alleviate some inequities and anomalies in the present income maintenance system and to provide a better standard of living for elderly people *now*.

Pensions

6 The level of the state retirement pension should be increased immediately to 33% of average industrial earnings for a single person and 50% of average industrial earnings for married couples. During the phasing-in period, changes would have to be made within the tax and supplementary benefits system so that no pensioner is worse off and real increases in pensions are ensured.

7 The link between pension upratings and average earnings should be restored. Upratings should take place at least twice yearly and there should be provision for more frequent upratings.

*8 The Government should initiate studies on a pensioner price index to replace the retail price index as the mechanism for adjusting benefit levels.

9 The time lag between the announcement of pension increases and their implementation must be reduced.

10 The earnings limit should be abolished so that retirement pensioners may earn as much as they are able without having their retirement pension reduced if they are men under 70 or women under 65.

*11 The retirement pension should eventually be paid to all on equal terms regardless of sex or marital status.

12 The condition should be abolished whereby a married woman who reached the age of 60 before April 1979 had to pay full national insurance contributions for at least half the years between the date of her marriage and reaching the age of 60 in order to qualify for any retirement pension on her own contributions.

*13 A thorough appraisal and full public debate should take place on the value of the contributory principle.

14 Pensions should not be dependent on a contribution record and all elderly people should receive the full basic pension. Early consideration should be given to increasing the rate of the non-contributory retirement pension for those over the age of 80 to the rate of the full retirement pension.

15 There should be an additional flat pension for those of 75 years and over, to be increased each year in line with rises in the retail price index. This pension should not be counted as income for supplementary benefit purposes.

16 Pension increases should be paid to those who live abroad even where they are resident in countries without reciprocal social security arrangements.

*17 A pension card should be provided to each pensioner to avoid the necessity of carrying a pension book as a means of identification for concessions.

*18 An additional pension should be given to those who have retired or will retire without full benefit of the earnings related pension scheme.

*19 Home responsibility protection should exist under the additional pension scheme for those looking after children or elderly parents.

*20 Contributions to both state and occupational pensions should be treated similarly for tax purposes.

Occupational Pensions

21 There should be more comprehensive coverage within the occupational pension structure. For example, pensions should be offered to all employees, death-in-service benefits made available to widows or widowers, and upper age limits for participation abolished.

*22 There should be no minimum age requirement or length of service limit to the preservation of pensions and all employees should have a right to the employer's contribution towards the retirement pension.

*23 All occupational pensions should move towards transferability and at a rate which will provide the same level of benefits in a new scheme.

*24 All deferred pensions and pensions in payment should move towards annual revaluation on the basis of the rise in average earnings.

*25 Legislation should ensure that there is no discrimination on grounds of sex or marital status in occupational schemes.

*26 Personal portable pensions should not be introduced to the detriment of company pension schemes but legislation should allow for the transfer of an occupational pension from a company to a personal scheme where the new employer has no existing scheme. Employers should be required to contribute to such personal schemes.

*27 All members of occupational schemes should have the right to full details about their scheme – including a brochure on entry – and to protection through credit insurance against the employer's possible insolvency.

*28 Government support should be given to specialist counselling agencies and there should be an independent arbitration service.

*29 Employers should not be the sole trustees of pension funds unless there is no practical alternative. There should be a register of trustees and member participation in the management of the fund.

Flexible Retirement

30 A flexible retirement system should be introduced over the next ten years, identifying for example, a wide band between 60 and 70, to be used as a retirement period. Legislation will need to be introduced to prevent discrimination on the grounds of age. Access to industrial tribunals should be available until that age.

31 The minimum pension age for men and women should eventually be equalised to the age of 60, and a full basic pension should be paid at that age.

32 Schemes for gradual retirement should be encouraged and investigation should take place into the possibility of half-work, half-pension schemes for people wishing to opt for part-time employment before retirement without loss of income.

Unemployment Benefit

33 Whilst state retirement pension is paid at a different age for men and women, older workers who are unemployed during a prescribed period prior to the age of 60 (women) or 65 (men) should continue to receive unemployment benefit until they are entitled to receive a retirement pension.

34 The abatement of unemployment benefit for those over 60 who have an occupational pension above a certain limit should be abolished.

*35 Automatic crediting for pension rights, without the need to 'sign on' as available for work, should be extended to women aged 55–60.

Taxation

36 The Age Allowance must be converted into a retirement allowance and raised annually in line with inflation. Amended tax relief should come into operation immediately upon reaching the age of retirement. This would end the anomalous position of single, widowed and divorced women aged 60–64 who are retired and yet cannot receive the higher tax allowance available to men and women over 65.

*37 The Widows Bereavement Allowance should be converted to a Bereavement Allowance and should be available to bereaved men.

*38 The Blind Person's Allowance and Dependent Relatives Allowance should be increased and thereafter uprated annually.

Disablement Income

39 Disabled elderly people should be eligible to claim certain benefits which at present are only available to younger disabled people.

40 The Mobility Allowance should be extended to those who become disabled after 65. Payment should not cease at the age of 75 but continue regardless of age as long as other qualifying conditions are fulfilled.

41 The present system of income support for those staying at home to care for elderly, sick, or disabled people is inadequate. Investigation should take place into the actual or potential loss of earnings to carers.

42 The Invalid Care Allowance should be extended to married and cohabiting women and raised to the level of unemployment benefit.

43 The criteria should be reviewed whereby Department of Health and Social Security doctors and medical boards assess people as medically unfit for employment or disabled for benefit purposes.

*44 The Attendance Allowance should be paid to those in local authority homes or sponsored by local authorities in private or voluntary homes.

*45 The time limits for claiming all disability benefits should be the same and the six months lapse before an Attendance Allowance can be paid should be reviewed.

*46 The length of time it takes to process the Attendance Allowance is unacceptable and every effort should be made to expedite decisions.

*47 A disability income should be introduced for those who need to retire because of ill health.

Death Grant

48 The Death Grant should be increased immediately to reflect its introductory value in 1949 and uprated annually in line with the retail price index.

49 Those very elderly people, who were over or near pension age when the present national insurance scheme started in 1948 and could not pay contributions, should receive the full grant.

Christmas Bonus

50 The Christmas Bonus, which is part of the income maintenance system, should be restored to its 1972 value and increased annually in line with the retail price index until such time as pensions are adequate.

Housing Benefit

51 In the long term there should be an integrated and comprehensive scheme of assistance with housing costs administered by one agency. This should include rents and lodging charges, mortgage repayments, rates, water charges, minor maintenance and heating costs. The scheme should provide help to all regardless of tenure, and should treat every claimant's capital in the same way.

52 In the short term, changes should be made to the needs allowance to take proper account of the extra needs and expenses of elderly and disabled people.

53 Calculation of benefit should be based on the total rent and rates of a household.

54 All benefits should be in the form of monetary payments unless the claimant prefers them to be paid directly to the landlord and rating authority.

55 The non-dependent deduction should be abolished and instead the actual contribution made to rent and rates by the non-dependent should be counted as part of the houeholder's income for assessment purposes.

*****56** All elderly and disabled people should be able to have a home visit and assessment.

*****57** More resources must be made available to local authorities for staff recruitment and training in Housing Benefit.

*****58** Housing Benefit sections must inform relevant departments that they are processing claims to avoid summonses and notices to quit, and pay compensation if they have breached regulations.

*****59** There should be an obligation on local authority staff to inform people if they might be eligible for Supplementary Benefit.

*****60** Claims from private and housing association tenants should be a priority and expedited.

*****61** The right to interim payments should be extended to all claimants where Housing Benefit represents a substantial proportion of the rent.

*62 If they wish, all pensioners should have the right to a weekly payment of benefit and an open girocheque or book of orders encashable at the post office.

*63 There must be an alternative to the split Housing Benefit Supplement, which discourages take-up and fails to solve the 'better off' problem.

Water Charges

64 Water rates, sewerage and environmental charges should be treated as necessary housing costs and be eligible for the same assistance as general rates.

65 There is a need to review the systems of charging by water authorities to bring about harmonisation and uniformity of practice.

Supplementary Benefit

*66 The state pension should be sufficient to live on without recourse to Supplementary Benefit. However, a 'safety net' must be retained for extraordinary expenses and situations.

*67 There should be a major revision and revaluation of the minimum scale rates to reflect modern life styles. Components should be included for refrigeration, holidays and telephones. Additional and single payments should also be regularly reviewed. All costs should be evaluated and uprated twice yearly in line with inflation.

*68 Consideration should be given to abolishing the capital limit which is a barrier to integration of the benefit system, and replacing it with a taper system. In the interim, the savings limit on eligibility to Supplementary Benefit and the disregard on savings for people claiming single payments are too low. They should be increased immediately and uprated annually in line with prices.

69 In the short term, provision should be made for those elderly people without pensions or on reduced pension, who are not entitled to claim Supplementary Benefit because their capital exceeds a certain limit but is insufficient to provide an income to live on.

*70 The earnings disregard should be raised to its 1975 value and increased in line with inflation. Consideration should be given to phased reductions of benefit where unemployed people are easing their way back into work.

*71 The value of the age addition for supplementary pensioners aged 80 or over should be restored to its 1971 purchasing power.

*72 The deduction from additional requirements made for the available scale margin should be abolished.

*73 The restrictive and stringent criteria used to assess entitlement to single payments should be reviewed and revised. Payments should be available for replacement of worn out essential clothing, defunct refrigerators and for the cost of labour for house repairs.

*74 The Government should reintroduce the flexibility that existed in the regulations prior to 1980 whereby single payments could be claimed by people whose income is marginally above Supplementary Benefit levels.

*75 Exceptional needs payments should always be processed quickly and should be available where there is a likelihood of damage or risk to health or safety for the elderly person.

*76 The long term rate of Supplementary Benefit should be extended to older workers who have been unemployed for more than one year and they should not be required to come off the Employment Register to receive this rate.

*77 Older unemployed women aged 55–60 should be entitled to the long term rate of Supplementary Benefit and neither they nor men over 60 should be required to register in order to receive that rate.

*78 Spouses' incomes should be disaggregated when assessing for Supplementary Benefit and each adult should have entitlement in their own right. The minimum scale rates and capital limits for couples should eventually be twice the rate for single people.

79 Home visits for benefit assessments should be generally available to retired claimants whether or not postal claim forms are in use.

Take-up of Benefits and Administration

*80 DHSS and local authority benefit staff must be properly trained so that they are thoroughly familiar with the regulations and have studied interview techniques and the special needs of those who are hard of hearing, have speech defects, who cannot read or write, or whose language is not English.

*81 There should be a move towards setting up a network of small local benefit offices which are easily accessible to elderly and disabled people.

82 A major and continuing publicity/information exercise should be undertaken by the Government to encourage the take-up of benefits and to assure elderly people about their rights and entitlements to benefit.

*83 DHSS and local authority staff must take an active role in information and advice giving and encourage the take-up of benefits by initiating and participating in take-up campaigns, providing more free phone services, benefit buses, and information stalls. They should be able to talk in day centres and clubs to increase elderly people's own knowledge and ability to help themselves, and each other, to know their rights.

*84 Supplementary Benefit Form A14N is illegible and must be improved immediately.

85 Supplementary Benefit regulations should be in clear and simple language and available to claimants, advisers and benefit officers alike. They should be inexpensive to buy, if not free. Codes of instruction relating to regulations for use by benefit officers should be similarly accessible to all and easily understood.

86 All general literature relating to benefits and the rights of the retired should be produced in simple easy language and be readily available at a number of distribution points including both Crown and Sub-Post Offices.

*87 A series of clear leaflets in simple language and large print should be produced by DHSS for elderly people and sent out regularly with new pension books.

88 Leaflets, forms and information about pensions, Supplementary and Housing Benefit should be available in a range of languages to cater for people from ethnic minorities or other groups whose language is not English.

EMPLOYMENT

89 Everybody should have the right to work in relation to their needs, capabilities and wishes. It should not be assumed that unemployment is worse for younger people than older workers for those as a consequence may experience long term poverty and despair.

90 At a time when the combination of technology and recession leads to less employment, opportunities exist to create greater flexibility in working lives. Shorter working weeks, longer holidays, job sharing, and a period of time off for everyone should be coupled with the opportunity for older people to go on working.

91 Age should not be used as a criterion for redundancy selection.

92 There should be no discriminatory upper age limits in job advertisements, selection of new employees, or selection of employees for promotion. When public authorities are seeking to become 'Equal Opportunities Employers', one criterion should be that there will be no discrimination on the grounds of age.

93 There should be no automatic age restriction on holding voluntary public office.

94 Disabled people who attend work centres should not be subject to enforced retirement.

95 Older workers should have equal opportunities for in-service training and retraining towards second careers. The design of training courses should be geared to people's needs.

96 Opportunities should be available for older workers to transfer to part time work or to take less arduous work before retirement without detriment to pension rights.

*97 Employers who introduce early retirement schemes should credit the employee with the years between early and normal retirement for occupational pension purposes.

98 Opportunities should exist for retired people to obtain part time work in sheltered workshops, and their views should be taken into account in decisions on payment and day to day management.

99 Employment Bureaux services which cater for the specific requirements of older workers are welcome.

*100 Government funded schemes should review the development of programmes in the light of the needs of older workers; entry requirements should not be more restrictive for them than for younger workers and all unemployed people should be able to participate in such programmes.

LOCAL GOVERNMENT

General

*101 The basis of local taxation should be broadened to include non-householders so that single, and often elderly, people do not bear a disproportionate share of the cost of local government.

*102 Any efforts to restrict local authority expenditure through reductions in the rate support grant, targets, grant related expenditure assessments and rate capping, should not lead to cuts in essential services for elderly people.

*103 Grant related expenditure assessments should be revised as they take no account of major factors which determine elderly people's need for services such as social isolation and the strength of local health services.

The Urban Programme

*104 The Urban Programme, which is a valuable aid in tackling inner city deprivation, must give priority to areas with high populations of very elderly, frail and poor people. Indicators of deprivation in later life must be defined and refined to identify their needs.

Abolition of Metropolitan Authorities

*105 Proposals to abolish the Metropolitan Authorities must not in any way reduce the quality and quantity of service provided for elderly people or affect the facilities to which they have access and the environment in which they live.

*106 Where necessary, safeguards given to the London concessionary fare scheme should be replicated for Metropolitan County transport. District/Borough Councils should be enabled to support such schemes without penalty.

*107 Metropolitan District and London Borough Councils should be able to help voluntary agencies previously supported by the GLC and Metropolitan Counties. The 2p rate which can be levied under Section 137 of the Local Government Act 1972 should be increased to 4p.

*108 Any joint boards established should include representatives from appropriate voluntary organisations.

HOUSING

General

109 Elderly people have a right to a high standard of accommodation where they can retain their independence and dignity as members of the community.

110 There is an urgent need to provide more accommodation of various kinds designed with the needs and wishes of elderly people in mind, particulary one and two bedroom housing, bungalows, ground-floor and sheltered accommodation. This need extends throughout the country and in all housing sectors.

111 All new housing should be designed to 'Mobility Standards', where practicable, to cater not only for those who are disabled at present but for those who may become so as they grow older.

112 Reductions in building and improvement programmes as a consequence of public expenditure cuts have led to serious housing problems, particularly in view of the increasing numbers of frail elderly people. As well as the need to build new housing, repairs and improvements to existing accommodation must be urgently accelerated.

113 Special provision in both the public and private sector is required for those with physical and mental disabilities and other individual needs. This should include not only extra-care sheltered housing, caring hostels and residential accommodation, but also the provision of housing and care services to elderly people in their own homes.

Housing Provision

114 There will continue to be an urgent need for local authorities and housing associations to provide suitable rented accommodation. This should consist of flats and smaller houses as well as sheltered housing. The design, location and management of newly built accommodation will need to reflect the increasing numbers of frailer elderly people.

115 Local authorities should use their power to seek exemptions from the Right to Buy in order to maintain their stock of housing particularly suitable for, and normally let to, elderly people.

*116 In its allocations to local authorities' housing investment programmes, central government should reflect the essential role of local councils in the provision of housing and related services. The close control imposed on local authority housing programmes should be relaxed to permit an element of choice in deciding local priorities.

117 Funding for housing associations, who play an important role in providing and developing housing, should be increased, and they should be encouraged to continue experiments in housing provision. Increased financial support for the voluntary housing sector should complement, not replace, public sector provision.

*118 The private sector should be encouraged to continue building smaller houses and bungalows for sale, to cater particularly for the requirements of elderly owner-occupiers seeking rehousing. Welcome should also be given to private sector builders who are now providing sheltered housing for sale.

*119 The Government should introduce a statutory system of registration and monitoring for private sheltered housing schemes to ensure that service provision and management are maintained to an acceptable standard.

120 Providers, whether in the public, voluntary or private sector, should ensure that the location of new housing for elderly people fosters links with the community. It should be near to shops, transport and other facilities and not entail a hill climb to obtain services.

*121 When designing special needs housing for elderly people, architects should pay special attention to the needs of those with physical and mental disabilities.

122 Public, voluntary and private bodies should combine to extend 'shared ownership' schemes to enable more elderly people with limited capital to obtain alternative housing. Housing associations and charitable organisations should be given the means to continue and expand leasehold schemes aimed at elderly people who cannot afford an outright purchase.

123 Co-operation between housing, health, social service authorities and voluntary bodies, both centrally and locally, is essential. In the case of existing conventional housing, this applies particularly to the provision of any appropriate aids and adaptations, the carrying out of any necessary repairs and the provision of personal domiciliary services where needed.

124 In the case of special housing provision, the need for co-operation additionally applies to its design, location and management particularly where extra-care facilities are provided either as an integral part of the scheme or through an input of extra domiciliary services. Joint finance should be available from the health service, whether for new extra-care schemes, or for projects to provide extra-care services for elderly people in their own homes.

Special Housing Provision

125 Local authorities, housing associations and other charitable and private housing bodies should ensure that the functions of their sheltered housing, hostels and other 'housing with care' schemes have been clearly defined and are continually reviewed.

*126 Encouragement should be given to extra-care sheltered housing schemes which enable elderly people to retain independence rather than having to move into residential care. Schemes involving shared finance between housing, health and social services departments are welcome and should be extended.

*127 Providers should seek to take extra-care services both to existing sheltered schemes and to elderly people in their own homes, so as to avoid wherever possible the need for an elderly person to move on to a special scheme due to a lack of appropriate services.

128 Elderly people who may be considering sheltered housing as an option should be given full and clear information about the varying facilities available in schemes, in order to make an informed choice.

129 Since the wardens are a key component in the effectiveness of sheltered housing, it is essential that they have an established policy for their scheme, a clearly defined job description, adequate payment, full support from their employers and the caring agencies and continuing training for themselves and their supervisors.

130 Communal facilities and extra-care services should be available to those elderly people resident in the community surrounding special housing. With the agreement of tenants who live in special accommodation, communal rooms should be available for use by local organisations to provide luncheon clubs or day centres and to provide educational facilities for the neighbourhood. This could help to ensure a balance of provision for sheltered housing tenants and those living in their own homes.

*131 Private sector developers of sheltered housing who are not experienced in the administration of housing schemes should hand over the day-to-day management to established housing associations. It is particularly important for both the sales literature and the lease to include details relating to matters such as tenure, equity, service charges and the warden's duties.

*132 Urgent consideration should be given to the provision of a warden service as a community resource to elderly people in their own homes as an alternative to traditional sheltered housing.

*133 Alarm systems are an integral part of sheltered housing provision. New systems should not be allowed to intrude upon the privacy of an old person. Alarm systems are never a substitute for caring relationships.

*134 There is a need for further research into the value and reliability of dispersed alarm systems for elderly people in the community. Such evaluation should take account of the views of elderly users. Prospective providers of such systems should carefully consider their objectives and pay greater attention to the quality of the response arrangements. Care should be taken not to impose on neighbours, volunteers and other informal carers.

135 There will continue to be a need to initiate and monitor experimental schemes for housing elderly people. This should be directly connected with research into their needs, so that services are provided as a response to those needs. The desire for extended family homes, including 'granny annexes' and specially designed large houses should be investigated. Experimental 'group-living' schemes both in the community and in residential care can be of value.

Access to Accommodation

136 An increase in the provision of new council housing should be accompanied by a relaxation of residence restrictions, to enable elderly people in all tenures to move across local authority boundaries for social reasons, often to be nearer relatives and friends. In such circumstances, local authorities should disregard length of residence.

137 Restrictions on owner-occupiers applying for council housing should be abolished. Councils should be able to buy properties from elderly home-owners in return for rehousing them in more suitable accommodation.

138 More consideration should be given to elderly people's need for housing mobility. The system of reciprocal transfers between local authorities should be extended. The quota of lettings made available under the National Mobility Scheme should be significantly increased to allow a special quota for elderly people seeking rehousing in another area. The current voluntary scheme requires legislation to ensure full participation. The Tenants Exchange Scheme should be publicised and simplified as much as possible.

139 To encourage further housing mobility, the transfer system within the voluntary housing association movement should be extended to include all associations nationally.

140 The provision and allocation of local authority accommodation should be evaluated in relation to the requirements of elderly people, such as their need for convenient, secure ground-floor or special housing, and their desire to be nearer relatives.

141 Public service agencies should have a clear policy for assessing the accommodation needs of frail and elderly people. Social service, health and housing authorities and other housing agencies should co-operate to ensure that the best assessment is made and the wishes of the elderly person considered.

Repairs and Improvements

142 There is the most urgent need to ensure that poor elderly households benefit from local authority grants for repairs and improvements. A major increase in the funds made available for home improvement grants should be accompanied by simplification of the grants system and greater publicity on the availability of grants. The Government should consider allocating grant aid according to the means and requirements of an applicant as well as the condition of the property but this must not result in increased bureaucracy which would deter elderly people from applying.

*143 The imposition of VAT on repair and improvement work should be abolished.

144 The limitation of repair grants to pre-1919 dwellings should be relaxed to take into account the problems of disrepair in later housing stock. Likewise more flexibility is required over the current limits on a property's rateable value. Grant conditions which allow only for substantial and structural repair work should be relaxed.

*145 Grants for rewiring should be made available immediately. Those who still have electric sockets with round holes in their homes should be entitled to a free check of the wiring system.

146 Central and local Government should promote and encourage voluntary initiatives regarding practical help for elderly people with repairs and improvements to housing. Assistance should be given to people on how to get advice from architects, surveyors and builders. Local authorities – acting on an agency basis – should consider taking on some repair work for elderly people who cannot cope with it themselves.

*147 Statutory, voluntary and private providers should be involved in helping elderly people redecorate their homes and obtain minor repairs. Schemes which exchange the skills of elderly people should be encouraged.

148 A regular, extensive and well publicised system of interest-only maturity loans is needed to help low income elderly home-owners to repair, improve or adapt their homes. Such loans should be available from local authorities and building societies should be encouraged to supply them. Lenders are urged to consider capitalising the interest payable, and to make available wherever possible smaller loans for minor repair work.

*149 Local authority expenditure on internal repairs and decorations should be concentrated on elderly tenants unable to carry out the work themselves.

150 More funds should be made available to local authorities and housing associations to enable them to carry out repair and enveloping programmes, particularly in the private rented sector.

151 The existing powers of local authorities should be strengthened and simplified to compel landlords to improve substandard property on a regular basis. In cases of genuine hardship, and, in particular, where there is an elderly landlord on a low income, local authorities should help landlord and tenant to find a solution to put the property into good repair including purchasing the property under their compulsory powers and rehousing the landlord and tenant.

152 Elderly people, their families and professional carers should be encouraged to take steps to ensure that accidents in the home are prevented wherever possible. Financial assistance should be available to elderly people who cannot afford to carry out necessary minor repairs and adaptations which would prevent accidents and therefore contribute towards the safety of the home.

Housing Advice

153 Clearer guidance is required on the housing options available to elderly people. Training for housing advice staff in voluntary and statutory organisations should include knowledge of their particular needs and those who work with them should also be aware of the range of housing options. The appointment of special housing advisers for elderly people in some local authorities is encouraging and should be developed.

154 Publicity material on housing information and services should be made widely available, particularly for elderly people who cannot or do not attend advice centres.

155 Guidance is required on the advantages and disadvantages of retiring to seaside and country areas, particularly with regard to the availability of shops, transport and other facilities and services.

156 Housing association schemes for elderly people should be widely publicised by both local and national housing agencies; and a central register should be kept of detailed information about the provisions of various schemes.

157 We welcome the initiatives taken by housing associations to provide alternative advice and help to those applicants who are ineligible for housing associations' property. They should receive funding to cover this work. Similar advice should be given by local authorities unable to rehouse applicants.

Homelessness

158 Elderly homeless people should be provided with permanent suitable accommodation including those who have special housing needs. This requires greater co-operation between housing, health and social service authorities in the assessment of, and provision for, homeless elderly people.

159 Temporary accommodation provided for homeless single people should be in small hostel units.

*__160__ There should be greater recognition that some elderly people remain far too long in residential care homes and hospitals because they are homeless.

161 Those people living in tied housing, due for retirement or retired early for reasons of ill-health, should never be considered as intentionally homeless under the Housing (Homeless Persons) Act 1977.

Tied Accommodation

162 Existing definitions of what constitutes tied housing are vague and unsatisfactory and a clear legal definition is required.

163 In certain circumstances of ill-health, early retirement or long service, suitable alternative accommodation should be provided for public sector tied tenants.

Mobile Homes

*__164__ Urgent steps are required to ensure that site owners abide by the terms of the Mobile Homes Act 1983, with particular regard to their obligation to provide home owners with a written statement outlining all conditions of occupancy.

AGE·CONCERN
PRICE LIST

TEA   per cup   10ᵖ

COFFEE   · ·   12ᵖ

TOAST   per slice   5ᵖ

with M...

75

*165 Further legislation is required to give pitch security to all home owners, and to allow them both access to information on, and the right to challenge, pitch rents and other site charges. The Government should closely monitor current arrangements regarding the resale of homes, paying special attention to site owners' right to claim commission on sales.

Mortgage Annuity Schemes

*166 The Government should initiate further investigations into schemes whereby elderly owner occupiers can raise capital and income using their homes as security. Financial institutions should consider ways of helping elderly people who are too young to qualify them for any of the current schemes.

Provision for ethnic minorities

*167 Providers of housing and services should make a specific commitment to meeting the needs of elderly people in ethnic minorities as part of an overall fair housing policy to be developed in conjunction with local community groups. For the policy to be 'fair' not only should the differing needs of various ethnic minority groups be recognised and provided for, but also the particular needs of elderly people within these groups.

*168 Providers should employ staff from ethnic minority groups in key positions, not just in specialist posts but as part of the general structure.

*169 Ethnic record keeping should be undertaken by those involved in providing housing and services, in order firstly to ascertain whether elderly people from ethnic minorities are making use of existing services, and secondly to ensure that providers are themselves implementing fair policies.

*170 Consideration should be given to making completely separate provision for ethnic elders of particular groups when this is requested. Providers should be flexible in their approach, but should ensure that they give special consideration to the particular needs of the potential occupiers.

HEATING

The Right to Warmth

171 Every person has a right to a warm well lit home. No-one should be prevented from having adequate heating and lighting or insulation in their homes as a result of excessive cost. The income of elderly people should be sufficient to meet their fuel costs.

172 The Government should undertake a full scale inter-departmental review in consultation with voluntary and welfare agencies to develop a national energy policy. This review should examine the methods available to provide help with heating costs for poorer consumers and to improve standards of insulation and energy conservation. The review should also examine the pricing policies of fuel industries and regional variations in the need for, and cost of, heating.

Heating Costs

173 Until the level of the pension is raised to be in line with average earnings, pensioners should receive a heating allowance to assist them in meeting the cost of heating and lighting their homes.

174 Fuel boards should abolish minimum attendance charges to pensioners for service calls.

175 Pre-payment meters should be available to all elderly people without additional cost and fuel boards should not refuse to replace prepayment meters in cases of theft. Meters should be designed so that users can assess when the meters need emptying and they should be positioned to give ease of access. Meters which are calibrated should be subject to a maximum limit on the unit price of fuel.

*176 The cost of warmth index may be an effective way of measuring the extent to which consumers are suffering from inadequate heat and light. The Government should fund a pilot project to assess its usefulness in practice, taking full account of regional differences in climate and the cost of fuels.

*177 Fuel costs should be taken into account in full in the assessment of Housing Benefit.

*178 Regulations governing single payments for fuel costs should be less restrictive.

Standing Charges

179 Standing charges for gas and electricity penalise elderly people who have a low fuel consumption. In recent years, these charges have increased at a faster rate than the unit cost of fuel causing considerable hardship to some elderly people. In future when considering price increases the fuel industries should place less emphasis on standing charges and more on unit costs.

Disconnections

180 The current Code of Practice does not protect consumers from hardship and individual circumstances are not always considered sufficiently when fuel boards decide to disconnect. It should be strengthened and made into a Statutory Code.

181 The power to order disconnections should be removed from the boards and given to county courts. It would be more equitable if fuel debts were collected through normal default procedures in these courts.

182 Pending the boards' power to disconnect being removed, the present protection for elderly people should be extended to the whole year.

183 A uniform policy must be developed throughout the country towards those consumers who have difficulty in paying their fuel bills. This policy must allow for repayment arrangements consistent with the financial resources of the consumer. It is essential that organisations representing consumers are consulted in the formulation of this policy.

Hypothermia

184 As the extent of cold related illness and deaths from hypothermia is a matter of great concern, heating allowances should be made available to all elderly people. Further research is needed into the living arrangements and bodily responses of people liable to be at risk in cold conditions. Any study should take into account the natural inclination of elderly people to economise on fuel and the importance of informing them of the danger of being cold.

185 The Departments of Energy, Environment and Health and Social Security should establish a common standard of minimum room temperatures acceptable for elderly people.

186 It should be a requirement that domiciliary and hospital nursing staff are provided with low-reading thermometers.

187 Local authorities should develop a more uniform and harmonised approach to the retention and distribution of heating appliances, aids and equipment.

Insulation

188 The system of grants for insulating dwellings up to the standard recommended by the Department of Energy should be extended to a national programme to insulate all dwellings. Any recognised deficiencies in existing grant schemes should be improved in the interim.

189 It is vital that sufficient resources are provided for voluntary neighbourhood energy and insulation schemes. All elderly and disabled people living in poorly repaired and insulated houses should have the opportunity to insulate their homes.

Services

190 Any closure of gas and electricity showrooms may reduce standards of service and might create difficulties for consumers. Reasonable alternative means must be made available for elderly people to pay their fuel bills at no extra cost to themselves. Safety standards must be maintained in servicing appliances.

191 Fuel stamps should be available at every post office and at as many other outlets as possible.

192 The needs of elderly and disabled people should be taken into account in the design of appliances, the development of easy-payment schemes and the methods of fuel debt collection.

193 Publicity should be readily available about services for the elderly consumer, including fuel advisory services. If necessary, home visits with repeat visits should be made to explain the use of appliances, easy payment schemes and the methods of fuel debt collection.

194 Fuel boards should ensure that their service engineers keep appointments to carry out repair work and that appliances are serviced as promptly as possible.

SOCIAL SERVICES

General

195 Social services are provided by statutory authorities, voluntary organisations, private agencies, families, friends and neighbours and collaboration amongst them is essential.

196 Given the key role of voluntary agencies in providing services, both national and local statutory bodies should consult with appropriate agencies prior to changing policies and administrative practices.

197 The aim of social policy should be for elderly people, including those in hospital and residential homes, to lead as full a life as possible including involvement in the local community.

198 As the number of very elderly people increases, additional spending will be necessary on existing statutory services which form the essential basis of their care.

*__199__ In placing increasing demands on the voluntary sector, statutory authorities must realise that some activities may not be appropriately met by volunteers. If new projects are envisaged, funding should be provided for them otherwise existing services may suffer as workers attempt to raise money for, and organise the new services. Core funding from the statutory authority must always be safeguarded to enable existing work to continue.

*200 In providing support to frail elderly people, rather than offering a standard and limited number of services, agencies should design a flexible range of services to meet the needs of the individual.

Financing Services

201 In order to guarantee adequate social service provision, the Government should establish minimum standards of provision for certain services based on the number of elderly people, taking into account the greater needs of very elderly people and their increasing number in the population. The criteria established should include deprivation among elderly people living in rural areas and inner cities. Money should be made available so that these minimum requirements can be adopted by local authorities who would then have a clear duty to meet the needs of individual elderly people.

202 Whilst local authorities charge for services, they should monitor the effect of this practice to make sure that those most in need are receiving help.

Home Helps

*203 Home helps are a fundamental service and should not be cut. They should be provided on the basis of social and medical necessity and without charge to the client.

*204 There is a sizeable unmet need for home helps and provision should be expanded. The service must be flexible in order to respond to an individual's changing requirements and should offer weekend and evening services. Local authorities should fully implement procedures for the regular reassessment of clients' needs in order to facilitate rehabilitation and reduce dependency.

205 Adequate cover must be available to provide a back-up service to people, if they want it, when their regular home help is absent.

*206 Written information should be provided to clients on the duties and relevant conditions of employment of home helps and details of complaints procedures.

*207 A home help should be able to provide the essential housework duties required by an elderly person.

*208 Consideration should be given to the role of the home help in the collection of pensions and benefits.

209 Guidelines should be established regarding the role of home helps as members of a caring social and health service team. These should be given to the home helps to enable them to deal with elderly people with special needs.

*210 There should be sufficient home helps and community nurses available so that neither need perform any task which requires the expertise of the other.

*211 Intensive home help or domiciliary aid services can make a valuable contribution to the care of frail old people. Local authorities should consider the case for such services but also recognise the need which many old people have for the traditional service providing domestic assistance.

212 Home helps should be provided for elderly people irrespective of whether a carer is resident or living nearby and the needs of carers should always be taken into consideration.

Meals Service

213 There should be a radical examination of the value of the meals on wheels service, including the nutritional value of the meal and its importance as a visiting service. It should be recognised that for the service to be effective some people require a meal seven days a week.

214 The provision of home freezers and frozen meals as an alternative to the traditional meals on wheels service gives elderly people greater independence and the freedom of being able to decide when and what they eat. Other nutritional support services, including mobile shops and the sale of food in day and social centres, should be considered.

*215 To avoid dependency on institutional meal services, collaboration should take place between local and health authorities, voluntary agencies and health education departments in running cookery and nutrition classes for older people who for various reasons lack basic skills. Schemes encouraging single people to cook for and dine with other people should be promoted.

216 Luncheon clubs make a significant contribution to the well being of elderly people on nutritional and social grounds, and should be widely available.

217 The underused buildings (including schools) that exist in many communities should be used to house luncheon clubs and other activities. Ways should be explored for elderly people to eat with children.

218 The provision of meals in institutions, in day centres and on wheels, and health education for elderly people should strive to improve nutritional standards.

Day Centres

219 There should be sufficient day centre places easily accessible for the growing number of elderly people, and a wide range of facilities should be freely available to those attending centres. Mobile centres should be provided in areas with no permanent or appropriate buildings where there is no transport to existing centres.

*220 Day centre care means different things to different people and the danger of assuming it is all things to all people needs to be avoided. Centres should clarify what their particular service offers and to whom. They may need to specialise in order to meet certain needs.

*221 Day centres must be planned within the context of the patterns of community care available within the area. They can provide a powerful growth point for a range of other services and activities in the centres or reaching out into the local community.

*222 Consideration should be given to providing day care to small groups in the private home of one of the attenders or that of an organiser.

223 Elderly mentally and physically frail people should have full access to day care, and additional trained staff should be provided to meet their needs.

*224 Day centres should be encouraged to explore ways of helping isolated and poor people, and charges should be monitored so that they do not act as a deterrent to those who would like to attend a centre.

225 Day care provision must be flexible, enabling elderly people to attend day centres whenever they like including weekends.

*226 Consideration should be given to how local authorities could monitor the increasing provision of day care by private agencies in order to protect the interests of frail elderly people.

227 Adequate and reliable transport is vital to enable the full use of day centres; and collaborative schemes should be established by statutory and voluntary organisations to provide a coherent transport service.

228 Residential homes should be used for day care services providing the residents are happy to open their Home to the community. This would benefit those people not living in Homes and would also help integrate residents into the wider community.

229 People who attend day centres should be fully involved in planning and organising their activities and services.

*230 Local Council Education and Leisure and Recreation Departments should offer their services in day centres.

Social Work

*231 Social work education must give greater emphasis to the process of ageing and the needs of elderly people.

232 It is essential that social workers collaborate with all those concerned with the welfare of elderly people – including housing, social security and voluntary agency staff, primary care teams, religious groups, and elderly people themselves and their families. Proper planning, management and constant evaluation of social work intervention will ensure the efficient and effective deployment of resources.

*233 Elderly people have the same right as others to qualified social work support. Social Services Departments should consider how they can fulfil that obligation. Assessment procedures at the point of initial contact should take account of people's possible requirements for social and emotional as well as practical support.

*234 Social workers have a range of skills which can help improve the quality of life of old people in difficulties. These include enhancing caring networks in the community and other forms of community work which build up the abilities and confidence of groups of elderly people to speak and act for themselves. It is essential that social workers are given reasonable workloads and adequate support to enable them to practise these and their individual counselling skills with old people to the highest possible standard.

235 Field social workers should participate in regular reviews of clients in residential care and provide support for their rehabilitation when appropriate in the community.

236 Experiments in different ways of using staff, including forms of specialisation should be encouraged in relation to social work support for elderly people.

Chronically Sick and Disabled Persons Act and the Provision of Aids

237 Local authorities who have not conducted a survey of disabled people have failed to fulfil their duties under the Chronically Sick and Disabled Person Act and should now give priority to undertaking this work.

238 Insufficient resources have been allocated for the aids and adaptations which should be provided under the Act.

*239 Aids and services provided under the CSDP Act are unequally distributed, unpublicised and provision is often poorly co-ordinated. Local authorities should attempt to remedy this by implementing the Code of Practice on Section 2 of the Act prepared by the group of national organisations, including Age Concern England.

*240 An adequate number of occupational therapists are vital to properly assess the functional environment of elderly people and their need for counselling as well as aids and adaptations. There should be an increase in resources for training supported by educational grants.

241 Where authorities are providing services outlined in the Act, such as the cost of telephone rental, they should not be allowed to withdraw assistance from existing recipients unless they no longer require a particular service.

242 A large number of local councils have failed to supply sufficient telephones to meet the needs of many sick and elderly people. The Government should consider ways of assisting with the installation of telephones and with the payment of telephone charges.

243 It should be a duty upon statutory authorities to provide a laundry service for clothes and bedding to all people suffering from incontinence.

244 Deaf, hard of hearing, partially sighted and blind elderly people face particular problems and need the services of specialised professional workers to help them come to terms with their disability and to secure assistance. Local authorities should consider how these needs can best be met.

245 Consideration should be given to providing consumer information on aids for disabled people, including consumers' experiences, results of trials and comparative costs.

246 There is an urgent need for an effective emergency repair service for broken aids, wheelchairs, artificial limbs, and other appliances such as hearing aids and dentures. Suppliers of special aids should provide advice on and training in their use.

Services for Ethnic Minorities

*247 Social services should respond to minority groups and professionals providing these services should receive training to enable them to be sensitive to the needs of these groups.

*248 Minority groups should always be consulted about their wishes and efforts should be made to ensure that there are members of such groups in key posts in the social services.

*249 In order to ensure that ethnic groups receive an equitable distribution of services, some form of ethnic monitoring of clients must be carried out.

*250 Maximum use of money under Section 11 of the Local Government Act 1966 must be encouraged to promote quality services for minority groups.

*251 Literature and posters describing available services should be prepared in such a way that people whose first language is not English can understand them.

*252 Meals in day centres and on wheels should offer a range of choice to cater for religious, cultural and dietary needs, even in areas where minority groups are rare.

*253 There should be day centre provision so that members of ethnic minorities meet their contemporaries from the same groups under acceptable conditions and are made to feel welcome.

*254 In order to develop the use of residential care facilities, positive encouragement should be offered when desired to minority groups including provision of special facilities.

Social Services and Voluntary Agencies

*255 Active steps should be taken to ensure good relations between professional bodies and voluntary agencies. These are essential in the development of new programmes and can provide an early warning system of difficulties and help to resolve them.

256 When local authorities appoint voluntary or community liaison officers they should, at the same time, maintain their level of funding to the relevant voluntary agencies.

Family Support

257 Those working with elderly people have a responsibility to 'family carers' and their continued support should avoid the situation where the caring relative/friend can no longer cope with the responsibility of care.

258 Unresolved grief can lead to medical and physical ill health. Bereaved people should be assisted through their bereavement by selected, trained, accredited and supported volunteers or, when necessary, by qualified social workers, psychologists or psychotherapists.

259 Provision of a variety of services by different authorities can be confusing to both elderly people and their carers. Consideration should be given to establishing the post of a 'link person' who would liaise with and provide information for carers. Statutory authorities could consider making special appointments of such people and involving them regularly in case conferences.

*260 Local and health authorities must provide services to relieve carers including holiday relief schemes, short stay residential care, sitting services, day care and individual packages of care. Consideration should also be given to how existing local authority services can be adapted to meet the needs of carers.

*261 Schemes should be available to place elderly people with families, particularly for short stays. Research should be undertaken into problems of long-term placements, including the question of remuneration of the carers.

Old Age Abuse

*262 Detailed polices and measures should be devised to reduce the extent of old age abuse and provide support to both elderly people and their carers. This will require a multi-disciplinary and co-ordinated response involving a wide range of agencies and the formulation of training programmes.

*263 Attempts should be made by all professions to identify elderly people at risk of abuse. The primary health care team should play a key part through use of age/sex or 'at risk' registers.

*264 Consideration should be given to the establishment and use of special procedures to reassure, protect and prevent abuse of, elderly people.

Entering Residential Care

*265 Elderly people have the right to remain in their own homes even if some degree of risk is involved. They should make this decision in full knowledge of the risks and the options available and should not be penalised by the withdrawal of services if they stay at home. There should be a sufficient level of community care for people to remain in their own homes if they wish.

*266 Some people prefer to go into residential care and admissions procedures should be sensitive to individual needs, with information and consultation available to people considering going into residential homes. All Homes should provide a booklet for elderly people and their families setting out the limits to care, illustrating the Homes and explaining the charging procedures. This should form the basis of a contract for all people going into Homes. They should be allowed to live in a Home for a trial period.

*267 In order to make a considered decision about entering a residential home, intensive domiciliary support should be available for those who suddenly need help because of the death of a carer or a deterioration in health.

*268 Facilities should exist for a multi-disciplinary assessment of all elderly people entering residential homes. It should be mandatory on local authorities to arrange such an assessment for their own Homes or when sponsoring in voluntary and private Homes. Social Security should also arrange assessment before providing financial support for those entering private and voluntary Homes.

*269 Regular re-assessment should allow residents to consider whether they would benefit from a change of accommodation and rehabilitation should be possible for those wishing to return to the community. Arrangements should thus be made to ensure that residents' own homes are kept available for an agreed time after they have entered a residential home.

*270 Elderly people should be able, if they wish, to live in residential homes near their relatives. It should therefore be possible to move into a statutory Home in an area other than the place of residence and also to move between Homes.

*271 There should be a uniform system of assessing charges for elderly people in local authority Homes, or sponsored by them in other Homes and for those in private or voluntary Homes who are supported by Social Security.

*272 It is essential that where Social Security enters into support for an elderly person in a private or voluntary Home that support should be continuous.

*273 Where a hospital or social service worker has placed an elderly person in a Home, the authority should accept responsibility for their funding in that Home if personal income or Social Security finance becomes inadequate.

*274 Where a person enters a residential home and their home is occupied by a relative or someone who has cared for them, it should form no part of the assessment of income.

275 Sponsorship by local authorities of elderly people in voluntary residential homes has played a valuable part in the provision of care and should continue with firmer national guidelines and a standardised system throughout the country.

276 Section 47 of the National Assistance Act 1948 which enables the Medical Officer of Health to compulsorily remove people from their homes into residential or hospital care is inappropriate in its present form and should be reviewed.

Residential Care

277 Increasing numbers of elderly people will require residential care. Provision of all types of accommodation should be increased and all new Homes should be sited near shops and transport.

*278 Private and voluntary Homes play a vital part in providing residential care and there should be close liaison and co-operation between this sector and the local authority.

*279 The recently enacted and strengthened legislation on the registration and inspection of private Homes is welcomed but local authorities must provide adequate resources to ensure that it is implemented.

*280 It is essential for local authorities to employ an adequate number of properly trained and supervised Registration Officers.

*281 A more realistic registration and annual fee should be charged to private Homes in order to cover the cost of inspection and advice given by local authorities.

*282 Stiffer penalties should be introduced for contravention of the new legislation.

*283 Monitoring should determine whether local and health authorities maintain an independent and impartial registration, inspection and advisory service for residential and nursing homes. If this does not take place the need for an independent national agency must be considered.

*284 The recommendations made in *Home Life: a code of practice for residential care* should be implemented in non statutory Homes and statutory Homes should be required to follow them in order to improve the quality of life of residents.

285 Greater consideration must be given to the quality of life in Homes. A primary goal should be that residents who wish may have their own rooms with bath, toilet and locking doors. They should be allowed to keep a quantity of personal possessions.

286 The officer in charge of the Home should ensure that regular reviews of the health and well-being of all residents are conducted.

287 A code of practice should exist for the treatment of money in residential homes, so that residents are enabled to cash their own pension and handle their own finances. As many services as possible should be brought to the Home so that people can spend the allowance. The local authority personal allowance should be increased to allow people to purchase their own clothes.

*288 Staffing levels in Homes need to be generally increased and training improved. Local authorities should offer training opportunities for private and voluntary Home staff.

289 Community nurses must be available at all times to meet the needs of elderly people in residential homes.

290 Specially designed short-stay Homes perform a valuable function in providing flexibility in meeting the care needs of elderly people and are more desirable than using places in ordinary residential homes for short stay.

291 The experience of living in small groups within residential homes can be an effective way of enhancing the autonomy of some elderly people in residential care. Provision of such accommodation for people who would benefit from it is recommended.

292 Board and lodging houses should be subject to registration and inspection when appropriate.

HEALTH SERVICES

293 As elderly people comprise the main users of the National Health Service they should be involved in the development of policies and the management of services. The current age limitations for people serving on health authorities should be abolished.

*294 The health care of elderly people necessitates collaboration between, and with, both the health and local authority services and voluntary agencies.

295 The work of Community Health Councils should be expanded and better funded. They play an essential role in representing consumers' interests and supporting individual complaints. Membership of voluntary organisations on CHCs should be increased and the interests of elderly people represented. The age limitations on membership should be abandoned.

Resources

296 Health authorities must allocate more resources, particularly in preventive education and community health services, for the care of elderly people in accordance with their priority status as defined by the Government.

297 The formula which governs allocation of money in the National Health Service must be replaced or substantially modified so that resource allocation is more sensitive to demographic trends, the changing medical and social needs of elderly people and primary health care requirements.

298 If the Government allowed joint funding to be maintained over a longer period of time, local authorities would not be discouraged from building more residential and day-care facilities.

Preventive Education

****299** Insufficient resources and attention are devoted to the preventive and health education roles of the NHS. Well-elderly and other clinics, pensioners' health days, health courses and community health initiatives make a valuable contribution to health education for elderly people and are appropriate activities for health authorities to fund.

300 All age groups would benefit from improved health education and each district health authority should appoint a team of officers, one of whom could develop specific programmes for young and older elderly people.

301 The health care profession should be involved in pre- and post-retirement education to help people anticipate and prepare themselves for retirement.

302 More research and greater consideration of its practical application should be given to normal ageing and medical conditions which occur in old age such as arteriosclerosis, arthritis, strokes, incontinence, dementia and depression.

General Practitioner Services

303 General Practitioners have a key role in determining the well-being and comfort of elderly people. GPs have a special responsibility to give elderly patients full and unhurried consultations as they are often the first point of contact.

304 GPs' training should take greater account of the special medical conditions, treatment programmes and changing social circumstances of elderly people.

305 GPs' records should be restructured regularly and age/sex registers compiled, and used as a check on those people most at risk. Annual check-ups should be offered to all elderly people, with special attention given to the very old, the isolated and those facing changing circumstances. The GP and his team should be encouraged to make follow-up visits to those who do not come for a check-up.

*306 Consideration should be given to ways of encouraging GPs to do work with older patients, particularly preventive work, including special payments for the practice.

*307 There should be a code of practice to guide GPs in their treatment of elderly people.

*308 GPs should be encouraged to make efficient, effective and economic use of resources in relation to prescribing and other major expenditure.

309 All GP surgeries should be comfortable and well equipped.

310 Health centres have the advantage of providing a range of primary care services under one roof. Centralisation of services may, however, create difficult journeys for elderly patients, particularly in rural areas. Health authorities should take responsibility for transporting elderly people to their nearest health centre.

*311 The use by GPs of deputising services should be kept under strict review by Family Practitioner Committees. Elderly people need continuity in service from a GP and every effort should be made to ensure that information is available to the deputising service and reported back to the patient's own GP.

312 Receptionists in surgeries have a key role to play and should be carefully recruited and trained so that patients have easy access to their GP. It should be possible to see a doctor without a pre-arranged appointment.

313 GPs should be prepared to collaborate in a multi-disciplinary team with other health and social service practitioners and voluntary agencies to encourage co-operation in primary care. While there is a strong case for a greater exchange of information between professionals, such a relationship must respect confidentiality and the wishes of the patient.

314 Immediate attention must be given to the lack of primary care facilities in the inner cities and other stress areas. Further resources must be made available to improve and replace run-down surgeries, and elderly single-handed GPs should be encouraged to take on assistants. Methods of providing care for 'homeless and rootless' elderly people should be explored.

*315 GPs should be more aware of the informal supportive networks of carers. They should consider the implications for their work of the fact that confused and frail elderly people may only be able to communicate with them through their families or friends.

Community Health Services

316 It is highly desirable that health care professionals and personal social service staff, including home helps and occupational therapists, work together closely as equals. This co-operation would be enhanced if more social workers were based in health centres.

317 Community nurses play a key role in primary care teams and their numbers should be increased. Consideration should be given to the greater use of auxiliary nurses under supervision and their role in relation to local authority staff should be reviewed to facilitate an effective service.

318 In the course of expanding their work in clinics, community nurses should maintain their critical domiciliary role. Night and weekend nursing and night sitting services all urgently require additional resources.

*319 Community mental handicap teams should be strengthened to enable them to play a supportive role for elderly mentally handicapped people returning to the community and for elderly people looking after mentally handicapped adult children.

320 As they work within the primary health care team, health visitors should be trained to take greater responsibility for the needs of elderly people. The value of specialist health visitors should be considered.

321 An expansion of the physiotherapy, speech and occupational therapy services in the community should be encouraged and adequate funding allocated. The DHSS should issue advice on the establishment of domiciliary services.

322 An increase in health care services, including community psychiatric provision, is necessary to cater for the growing number of elderly mentally frail people being cared for outside hospitals.

323 The community psychiatric nursing service should be expanded with nurses based not only in hospitals but also attached to health centres. The initial assessment of mentally frail people should always take place in their own homes.

324 Geriatric day hospitals and psychiatric day hospitals play a useful role in assessment and rehabilitation. Their use as day centres should be questioned.

Medicines and Pharmacy Services

*325 Older people's use of medicines should be much more closely monitored at all stages from initial prescribing, to dispensing, the consumption of the medicine, and at any subsequent phases of the therapy. Hospitals must monitor their drug therapy for elderly people and ensure that the programme is co-ordinated when the patient is returned to the community. This requires close liaison between doctors, pharmacists, carers, and other members of the caring team and older people themselves. Systems should be established to reduce overprescribing, long term medication and reliance on repeat prescriptions. As a minimum doctors should be required to conduct an annual review of the drugs being taken by their elderly patients.

*326 More information and education about the intended benefits and likely adverse effects of medicines is needed by individuals and those involved in their care both as general knowledge and in relation to current or potential treatments. These should be provided by prescribers themselves, pharmacists and a range of health educationalists.

*327 There should be a statutory requirement to monitor the effects of drugs on all age groups. This would include test trials not only for new drugs but also medicines which are already in use. Specific advice in prescribing a drug for the elderly should be included on manufacturers' drug data sheets. Doctors and pharmacists should carefully monitor the use of new drugs for older patients and report any suspected adverse or inappropriate reactions to the Committee on the Safety of Medicines which should have amongst its members experts in the medical care of older people.

*328 Efforts should be made to draw attention to, and reduce, the high level of use of hypnotics by older people. More education is needed about normal sleep patterns in later life and about regimes and lifestyles that reduce the need for hypnotics.

*329 Memory aids can be useful in helping elderly people to take drugs as and when directed. When this is the case, they should be available free of charge on the National Health Service.

*330 Pharmacists should take a greater role as health educators and advisers to the public on use of medicines on minor complaints and in encouraging more discriminate use of over the counter medicines. Pharmacies should accordingly be arranged to facilitate relatively confidential consultations. Pharmacists should also be enabled to make domiciliary visits to clients' homes to give advice and encouraged to adopt an outreach approach to their work, to give talks and advice to groups of pensioners in a variety of settings.

*331 All elderly people should have access to a pharmacist and consideration should therefore be given to how an appropriate geographical and numerical spread might best be achieved offering incentives, including finance in the form of an initial allowance or reimbursement of expenses.

*332 Residents in sheltered housing schemes, residential care and nursing homes should have their medicines dispensed on an individual basis. The bulk prescribing of 'prescription only medicines' should be prohibited.

*333 Consideration should be given to the implementation of the Greenfield Committee's recommendation that pharmacists should dispense generic drugs instead of branded ones unless the GP has indicated otherwise on the prescription form.

*334 Greater information should be available to prescribing doctors about drugs, their therapeutic uses and their implications for elderly people.

*335 Some illnesses or health related problems for which drugs are prescribed may be tackled more appropriately through education, by other help such as counselling, nutritional advice or by addressing underlying social, economic and environmental conditions. Education is required to ensure that neither the professional nor the patient has an excessive misplaced faith in the efficacy and safety of drugs.

Chiropody

336 Chiropody, a key service to many elderly people, must receive a greater allocation of resources. Priority should be given to meeting the shortage of chiropodists and grants for students wishing to achieve qualification should be made mandatory.

337 A more uniform system of pay and conditions should be established for chiropodists in the state and private sectors.

338 Footcare and normal nailcutting schemes, closely supervised by experts, can make a substantial contribution to overall provision. Professional chiropodists should be encouraged to co-operate with voluntary organisations who can help elderly people with footcare. Voluntary schemes and unqualified footcare assistance should not, however, be seen as substitutes for an increase in the number of qualified chiropodists.

339 Chiropodists should provide more domiciliary visits and also undertake greater outreach work providing care and health education in a variety of settings.

Dental Services

340 Urgent consideration must be given to the problems which a sizeable number of elderly people face in finding NHS treatment, especially over the supply of dentures.

*341 Dental training should include study of the special needs of elderly people, and dentists should be encouraged to work with elderly patients. Consideration should be given to the need for a special fee or a salaried dental service.

*342 Domiciliary visits should be more readily provided on the National Health Service. Dentists should be encouraged to develop an outreach approach which provides treatment in a variety of settings including health and community centres and in mobile dental surgeries.

*343 Grants and loans should be available to dentists who need to improve access to their surgeries.

*344 All pensioners should receive free treatment. Until this is available dentists should be required to display in their waiting rooms a list of current charges, details of eligibility for free or reduced rate treatment and how it can be obtained, sources of advice for people with problems in paying for treatment, and a statement that all treatment which is clinically considered necessary is available under the NHS.

*345 More dental technicians should be recruited as a matter of urgency. They should be better integrated into the dental care team and their pay, conditions and career structure enhanced.

*346 Improved dental care should be provided to long-stay hospital patients and a review of their current needs conducted. All dentures should be permanently marked at the time of manufacture.

Services for Ethnic Minorities

*347 Health services must be responsive to the needs of minority groups, including their cultural and religious practices at the time of death which must be respected. Health professionals must be trained to consult with, and respond sensitively to, minority groups.

*348 Where religion or custom demands, women should be able to receive care from doctors who are women.

*349 Health professionals must have knowledge of the diseases to which ethnic minorities are prone, and the appropriate forms of treatment. Education should enable ethnic groups and individuals to develop self care programmes.

*350 Meals in hospitals should offer a range of choice to cater for religious, cultural and dietry needs, even in areas where ethnic minority groups are rare.

*351 The right to NHS treatment for all people living in Britain should be fully explained particularly to members of ethnic minorities.

Services for Deaf and Hard of Hearing Elderly People

*352 The needs of deaf and hard of hearing elderly people are often neglected and require a co-ordinated and multi-disciplinary response.

*353 Trained and supported volunteers can play a vital role in complementing the work of professional staff. The Government should establish guidelines on projects for the hard of hearing.

*354 Priority should be given to reducing the considerable waiting times for NHS hearing aids. This can be caused by lack of staff and unnecessarily complicated procedures. Consideration should be given to establishing and implementing staffing norms and to determining the basic procedures that should be followed before an aid is dispensed.

*355 Hearing therapists can play an important part in maintaining the use of hearing aids by new users. In order to reduce the current shortage consideration should be given to the required number and role of hearing therapists and adequate funds must continue to be available to train them.

*356 Publicity material for elderly people on hearing loss should emphasise what a hearing aid can achieve and warn people that NHS aids can be just as adequate as those supplied privately. The services offered by commercial suppliers should be closely monitored by health authorities to safeguard against malpractice.

*357 Information should be readily available about environmental aids for deaf and hard of hearing people, and where they can be obtained. Consideration should be given to whether there should be an allowance or grants for all types of aids, rather than just issuing free NHS hearing aids.

*358 Prelingually deaf people have particular needs which should not be confused with those of deafened people. In allocating residential accommodation care should be taken to maintain and create groups of prelingually deaf people so that they can communicate with each other.

*359 Greater information should be made available locally on the provision of lip reading and where appropriate signing classes which should be within the means of all who are handicapped by impaired hearing. By their nature lip reading classes must be small and therefore they should not be expected to meet the same criteria about numbers in class as other courses. The Departments of Education and Health and Social Services should determine a national policy on responsibility for teaching lip reading.

Needs of Blind and Partially Sighted Elderly People

*360 Free spectacles should be available to all elderly people who should be encouraged to take advantage of the annual free eye sight test in order to facilitate the early detection of sight disorders. Where necessary treatment should be available in elderly people's own homes.

*361 The procedure for registering blind and partially sighted people with the local authority should be both simplified and made faster to ensure that all relevant people receive the necessary information and waiting times are reduced. Counselling should be available to clients at the time of registration.

Fitting an inductive coupler, a simple device which clarifies speech and provides a clearer line for people with hearing aids.

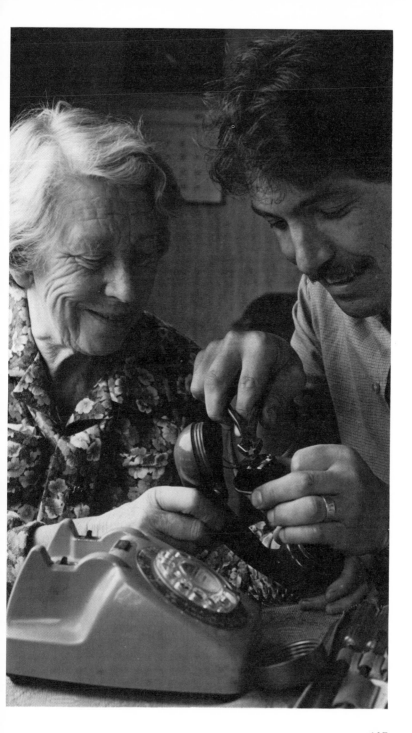

362 Low vision aids and services should be more readily available and key staff trained in their use. Free aids should be available not only through hospitals but also through high street optician shops.

363 The design of hospitals and residential homes and the training of staff should take account of the special needs of the blind and partially sighted.

Mental Illness

364 Elderly people may suffer from various forms of mental illness including dementia and depression. Each patient should receive a joint assessment and diagnosis from a psychogeriatrician and a geriatrician.

365 Each health district should, as a matter of urgency, establish an adequately resourced, co-ordinated and planned specialist service for psychiatry in old age involving close liaison and co-operation with social service, housing and voluntary agencies.

366 A consultant with responsibility for psychiatry in old age should be appointed in each health district to lead the specialist department, thereby fulfilling official DHSS policy.

367 In-patient hospital services should give priority to the most seriously mentally ill and those requiring specialist treatment.

368 GPs must consider how they can best meet the needs of elderly mentally infirm people and they must also be able to draw support from the district service. Both social service and health community services in many areas require further development.

369 Social service departments play a vital role in supporting mentally ill old people and should consider how needs can best be met. Each department should appoint an officer within its management team to have special responsibility for such services.

*370 More residential places should be set aside for elderly mentally ill people and in providing residential and nursing home care, the domestic character of the Home should be maintained for the benefit of mentally alert residents. The balance between mentally ill and alert residents should be carefully considered.

371 Greater priority should be given to research into the causes and treatment of dementia.

Care of the Terminally Ill

372 There should be a review of current provision for the terminally ill whether they live in institutions or have remained in their own homes. The introduction of the hospice concept in institutions or into the home, within the National Health Service is welcome, and all district health authorities should ensure adequate provision.

*373 The most advanced techniques of pain control should be available throughout the health service.

Management for Continence

374 Relevant health and social service staff should receive training in management for continence, and each health district should appoint a continence nursing adviser. There should be routine investigation of the causes of every patient's incontinence. Recommended methods of personal protection should be freely available for those who suffer from incontinence. Community health education should devote more attention to this issue.

Hospital Services

375 Demographic changes inevitably mean that elderly people will make greater demands upon hospital services. Their need for acute treatment, assessment, rehabilitation and long stay care must be given priority in the allocation of resources.

376 Assessment and rehabilitation procedures should take place in geriatric and psychiatric units based in district general hospitals. Proposals to reduce the number of geriatric and psychiatric beds in these hospitals must be reversed.

377 The shortage of hospital beds for elderly people must be overcome and new targets should be established which take account of the increase in the number of people over the age of 75.

378 Elderly people are entitled to all forms of acute medical treatment which can make a major contribution to their independence and mobility. They should not be denied surgery on the grounds that they are too old.

379 Close co-operation must be promoted between geriatric, psychiatric and other hospital departments so that patients may be placed under necessary supervision for recovery and rehabilitation once acute treatment has been completed.

*380 Methods of treating acutely ill people in their own homes should be researched and developed.

Long-stay Hospitals

381 Long-stay patients should be cared for in local hospitals which serve the needs of all the community. Such hospitals should receive full support from geriatricians and psychiatrists and should be used in training medical students and nurses.

*382 The quality of life for long-stay patients in both mental and geriatric hospitals must be improved. They are entitled to respect for their individuality. Consideration should be given to single rooms for those who would like them.

383 Medical and social service staff in hospitals should continually assess long-stay patients for rehabilitation into the community.

*384 As the old and usually geographically isolated mental and geriatric hospitals are closed, they should be replaced by small localised units. In transferring patients to the community in order to close long-stay hospital provision, consideration should be given to the needs of future generations of frail elderly people and those currently living in the community who would benefit from long-stay provision.

*385 Serious consideration should be given to the development of long-stay care and the feasibility of maintaining elderly people in the community throughout their lives.

*386 An equitable system must be devised for paying for long-stay care whether in hospital, residential or nursing home.

387 Hospital services for elderly mentally infirm people are severely deficient and must be improved. Psychiatric units for the elderly must be established in each locality, and targets met for the appointment of psychiatrists with a special interest in elderly people.

Discharge and After-care

*388 Discharge from all departments of the hospital and after-care procedures must involve close liaison between hospital, social services and voluntary agencies. Particular attention should be paid to the availability of informal carers and consideration should be given to their needs. One person should be given responsibility for co-ordinating after-care.

389 Convalescent facilities must be available to all elderly patients who require them.

Nursing Homes

390 The development of NHS nursing homes is welcomed but should be carefully assessed before further development.

*391 Recent measures to enhance the powers of health authorities are welcomed. Nevertheless, in order to establish a stricter system of registration and inspection, a realistic registration fee should be set. If monitoring shows that health authorities are not impartial in their judgement, the case for an independent agency should be reconsidered.

392 The DHSS should seek to improve the quality of life in nursing homes. This could be achieved partly through the involvement of voluntary agencies in visiting and inspecting Homes.

Patients' Money

393 The accumulation of patients' money in long-term balances is unacceptable unless this is part of the patient's own considered savings plan and this situation must not continue. A greater range of services and facilities should be available to patients and whenever possible they should be able to control their total weekly income.

394 Increased staff time should be allocated to advise patients who have difficulty in organising their own finances. Proposals are welcome for establishing independent agencies to assist them.

395 There should be no obligation on patients to be involved in group expenditures, and where patients' clubs are established they should be independently monitored.

Complaints

396 Further strengthening is required to the hospital complaints procedure regarding medical treatment and the possibility of an independent assessment within the existing procedure should be considered as should the setting up of an advocacy service for patients.

Industrial Disputes

397 Essential services for patients should be maintained by staff during industrial disputes. The guidelines published by the Volunteer Centre on the role of volunteers have the support of both trade unions and voluntary organisations and should be used.

Ambulance Service

*__398__ The ambulance service must be expanded with additional resources and better co-ordination so that bunched appointments and long waits are avoided. Health and local authority transport services should be closely co-ordinated. Criteria for the use of ambulance services should be based on social as well as medical needs; and non emergency services should be adequately resourced.

Staff and Training

399 The staff/patient ratios in most geriatric services are too low, and the DHSS guidelines are not being met. Priority must be given to correcting these deficiencies. Active steps should be taken to encourage staff to take up geriatric and psychiatric medicine and nursing. A nationally organised nursing recruitment drive should be launched.

400 Health care professionals should receive some multi-disciplinary training involving courses on the special needs of the elderly and training should occur in a variety of different settings including small hospitals and residential homes.

*401 The Vocational Training Scheme for those entering General Practice should include a compulsory period in geriatric medicine and psychiatric care of elderly people. There should be more rotating appointments for junior doctors involving geriatric training in long-stay hospitals.

Complementary Medicine

*402 Some complementary medicine therapies can make a major contribution to the well-being of older people and complement rather than replace orthodox medicine. Greater information on complementary medicine should be available to older people.

*403 Improved understanding of complementary medicine therapies should be promoted among conventional medical practitioners and dialogue between the two approaches encouraged. This should be reflected in the training of all medical staff.

*404 Methods of co-operation and collaboration between conventional and complementary medicine should be established. Older patients must not be penalised by their GPs if they use complementary therapies.

*405 Complementary medical therapists and practitioners should be state registered and independently regulated. Members of the public should thereby be protected from unqualified practitioners. The advertising of complementary medicine and products should be controlled.

TRANSPORT

General

406 Elderly people have a right to expect maximum mobility. It is essential that there is a firm commitment by statutory authorities to ensure that elderly people are not isolated and lose their independence through lack of transport.

Travel Concessions

407 In view of the wide disparity in the availability and types of travel concessions throughout the country, a national scheme of uniform concessionary fares should be introduced for both road and rail travel services in off-peak hours.

*408 Concessionary fares should be available for everyone over the age of 60.

*409 Proposals to open local authority bus services to competition from private operators should not lead to reductions in the value of concessionary fares.

Public Transport

410 Many elderly people are unable to travel freely, particularly in rural areas. Local authorities should ensure that sufficient passenger services are provided by public or private companies to meet transport needs.

411 Regular and co-ordinated bus and train services are essential to enable elderly people to travel.

412 More information and advice should be available for disabled people on the transport facilities that do exist and how to use them.

413 Local and national transport authorities should ensure that the safety standards of their services enable elderly people to travel at will in safety and comfort.

414 Where bus regulations instruct the crew not to move until passengers are safely on the bus, the same principle should be extended to apply to elderly and disabled people who should be seated before the vehicle moves.

415 A safety device on electrically operated doors should be made compulsory on one-man buses.

416 Transport authorities and operators should reconsider the design of buses, trains and coaches to provide for easier entry by elderly and disabled people. All future stock should be designed in consultation with elderly and disabled people and organisations representing them.

417 A lower entry step and internal split steps should be added to existing buses.

418 The practice of designating seats for elderly and disabled people is welcome and should be more widespread in both buses and trains.

419 Wherever possible a shelter with seating should be provided at every bus stop, and the planning of new routes should take this requirement into account.

420 Parking restrictions near bus stops must be strictly enforced so that buses are able to park close to kerbs.

421 Bus companies should conduct regular assessments of the quality of service provide by bus crews, and greater attention should be given in training of drivers to the special needs of elderly people.

422 The adequacy of luggage handling arrangements at British Rail stations, ports and airports should be urgently investigated with a view to ensuring that sufficient numbers of porters and luggage trolleys are available.

423 Help should be available to aid elderly people negotiating steps at railway stations, ports and airports and wherever possible ramps should be provided.

424 Given the increasing numbers of elderly people who use long distance bus and coach stations and airports, arrangements for luggage handling at such places should be improved.

425 More seats should be provided at railway stations for persons waiting for trains and meeting others.

426 All large stations should have at least one telephone kiosk for disabled people and one amplified handset. Public address systems should have loop facilities for people who are hard of hearing.

Alternative Transport

427 The development of alternative transport schemes designed to cater for specific needs is welcome. However, these schemes must operate to complement the exisiting local and national transport system instead of replacing it. Alternative schemes must be funded adequately by central and local Government.

428 The Government should give relief from VAT for minibuses purchased by voluntary organisations.

Road Safety

429 The time allowed for elderly people to cross roads on crossings controlled by the 'Green Man' automatic system is totally inadequate. Relevant authorities must ensure that elderly people are able to cross safely and research into the most appropriate ways of achieving this is welcomed.

***430** The Government should establish more generous standards for pedestrian crossings so that greater importance is given to the need for people to cross in safety. It should advise motorists and cyclists not to start moving until people have reached the pavement at the other side of the crossing.

431 A disproportionate number of elderly pedestrians are involved in road accidents. We urge local and national transport authorities in consultation with voluntary organisations, to consider ways to alleviate the dangers faced by elderly people.

432 For ease of access for elderly people ideally all new roads should be planned with crossings at ground level rather than by subway or bridge.

433 Good street lighting and well maintained roads and pavements are essential to safe walking, particularly for elderly people. Local authorities must not cut these vital services.

434 Every pavement should have dropped kerbs to allow for easy movement of wheelchairs and invalid carriages.

435 Legislation should be introduced so that pavements are kept free from obstruction. A more stringent eye should be kept on cars parked on them and 'free standing' advertisements should be banned.

CRIME

436 Measures should be taken to reduce the level of crime, especially violent crime against elderly people.

437 'Community Policing' experiments must be pursued more vigorously so that the general public becomes more aware of the safety of their elderly neighbours and more alert to assisting the police by promptly reporting crime or suspected crime.

438 Neighbourhood watch schemes can play a valuable role in protecting elderly people against crime.

438 More 'beat' policemen must be seen patrolling the streets in high crime areas to give elderly people confidence to move outside their homes.

440 There should be more public education of elderly people in taking effective precautions against crime.

*441 Victim support schemes are of great value to elderly people who have been the victims of crime and should be adequately funded both nationally and locally.

ELDERLY PEOPLE AS CONSUMERS

442 Elderly people face particular problems as consumers because of their low income and restricted mobility. They should be protected by policies which aim to give easier access to goods and services and greater freedom of choice.

443 The rights and obligations that apply under the Sale of Goods Act should be extended to services.

444 Although elderly people may have less individual spending power, corporately they represent a very large section of the consuming public. Manufacturers and retailers of goods should attempt to cater for their particular needs.

*445 Consumer Councils have a vital part to play in the nationalised industries and elderly people should be represented on them. Councils should be independently staffed and given full access to information; they should serve the same function for each industry and be allowed to exercise greater influence in the development of policy.

Information

446 Although housebound people may benefit from services delivered to their homes, they are also vulnerable to uninvited doorstep salesmen and to the anxieties caused by the receipt of unsolicited goods and promotional material through the post. More information needs to be publicised about manufacturers' guarantees and their legal obligations.

Shopping

447 Managers of shops and stores should take into account the needs of elderly and disabled people. For example, provision should be made for an uncluttered store layout and for goods to be displayed within reach. Stores should provide seats for customers and checkout points for those buying a few items only. Even in large stores frail customers should be able to get individual service.

*448 The design of shopping centres should provide ease of access with adequate lifts, lighting, toilets, slopes whenever possible instead of steps, shutters or automatic doors and parking spaces for disabled people in car parks.

*449 Supermarkets should select a range of basic foodstuffs and apply a more equitable pricing strategy to ensure that purchasers of small quantities are not penalised. Self selection of fruit and vegetables enables elderly people to buy in small quantities and should be widely used.

*450 There should be an adequate number of enquiry points in stores.

451 All items for sale should be effectively labelled with essential information, set out in sufficiently large type and easy to understand. Packaging should be designed for easy opening by elderly customers and devices for opening containers made more widely available.

452 The decline of local shops which are situated near elderly people's homes and provide essential personal service is regretted. Legislation is required to prevent the 'change of use' of basic shops such as grocers and pharmacies. Councils should consider the possibility of financial support for neighbourhood shops and for mobile shops and services in their communities.

*453 In the treatment of suspected shoplifters, retailers should be careful to distinguish between those who intend to steal and those who are confused.

*454 Delivery of services to the home, including milk and post, are valuable and should be safeguarded.

*455 Elderly people need an easily accessible post office so that they can collect their pensions and pay bills. The Government and the Post Office must ensure that these facilities are available and that Sub-Post Offices, which provide a wider range of services, are kept open – especially in rural areas. This social value of the local post office should not be sacrificed to financial targets.

*456 Customer services in post offices – particularly the postal order service – should take into account the special needs of elderly people. Counters in Crown Post Offices should have at least one window fitted with a loop system for customers who are hard of hearing.

457 Local Chambers of Commerce and Trade should produce lists of the names and addresses of shops which carry a variety of goods and fittings of special use to elderly people.

458 The development of shopping clubs and self-help co-operatives is welcome.

*459 All food should be exempted from VAT.

Bank Services

*460 Banks should consider providing free banking services to elderly people and a wider range of financial services to those with limited resources at a reasonable charge.

*461 Building societies should be allowed to offer various financial services including paying bills, cheques and personal loans.

*462 Building societies and banks have an obligation to ensure that elderly people understand that tax paid interest will not be reclaimable.

Telephones and Television

463 Elderly people should have sufficient income to purchase, licence and maintain a television set.

464 All elderly people should be able to afford a telephone. The standing charges for residential users should be abolished in favour of higher call charges.

465 British Telecom should reconsider its pricing policy which has increased the cost of telephone calls and rental for residential consumers.

466 Public telephone kiosks should be kept in working order. They should not be closed without thorough consideration of the needs of the communities they serve, particularly in rural areas.

*467 When there are a number of telephone booths together at least one should be provided for disabled people and one with amplified handset for people who are hard of hearing.

PETS

*468 In view of the social benefit of pets, provision should be made for them in sheltered housing and institutions.

*469 Decisions about whether to keep pets should be dealt with on an individual basis between the tenant and the landlord rather than through restrictive rules.

*470 Veterinary treatment should be exempt from VAT.

EDUCATION AND LEISURE

General

*471 The distinction drawn between leisure and work is arbitrary and entirely individual. Positive encouragement should be given to elderly people to use the period of retirement to further their education, pursue recreational and cultural interests and give service to others.

472 An elderly person wishing to pursue an interest or activity – whether it be educational, recreational or cultural – has as much right to pursue that activity as any other member of the community. They should be able to share facilities available to the community with others, or if they wish, separately.

Facilities

473 Local authorities or other Government sponsored bodies, having identified the preferences of elderly people, should develop and publicise local facilities which meet their varied interests and ensure a more even level of provision of educational and leisure activities.

474 Where necessary elderly and disabled people, particularly in rural areas, should be provided with transport to enable them to pursue recreational and educational activities.

475 Those responsible for educational and leisure facilities should be urged to ensure that elderly people are not denied full use of these because of lack of provision for special needs – such as, suitably located and sufficient toilets, resting places, facilities for making drinks, access for the disabled and assistance for the hard of hearing, partially sighted or blind.

476 Small, local activity centres which are readily accessible and in familiar surroundings are invaluable to elderly people who, through restricted mobility and lack of confidence, do not use large adult education or leisure centres. Existing facilities must be safeguarded and further provision encouraged.

*477 Multi-use of all community facilities is essential. Educational premises including universities, colleges and community schools can give wider opportunities for elderly people and allow them to work with schoolchildren, older students and others, sharing their knowledge and learning with each other. Particular attention should be paid to daytime use of empty classrooms and wherever possible community facilities should be open to elderly people in the holidays.

478 Local authorities should support self help groups of elderly people to organise their own education, entertainment and recreational activities by the provision of premises, equipment, advice and financial help.

479 Holidays give an essential break from the normal environment and routine. We welcome the special holiday schemes for elderly people managed by commercial and voluntary organisations and by social services departments.

Education

480 Local authorities should ensure that sufficient opportunities are available for pre-retirement education, whether provided by employers, voluntary organisers, trade unions or themselves.

*481 Pre-retirement courses should give greater emphasis to the value of leisure activities and to emotional relationships.

482 When employers do not provide pre-retirement courses, they should give their employees day release to attend such courses.

483 The Government should call on local authorities to submit plans for the development of retirement education and provide for a crash programme of expansion in pre-retirement education.

484 All local education authorities should provide an adequate range of adult courses at suitable times of day and should ensure that fees are kept at a level which allows retired people to attend whatever classes they desire.

485 The staff of local education authorities should receive training in the educational and recreational needs of elderly people and how to develop activities for them.

486 Local authorities should encourage the development of networks of retired people with mutual interests.

487 When counting numbers for viable classes, local authorities should not treat elderly people as half persons because they are paying reduced fees.

*__488__ Local authorities should consider offering reduced fees for educational classes to people over the age of 60.

489 Adult education classes should be held at times which are convenient for elderly people to attend.

490 Learning opportunities must be attractive to elderly people with no previous involvement in any form of post-school education.

491 Elderly people should be given the opportunity to pass on their knowledge of traditional crafts and skills as well as their experience of recent history.

*__492__ Organisations developing and promoting learning and leisure opportunities through all media forms and those using distance learning techniques should consider the requirements of elderly people.

*__493__ Local authorities should consider seconding leisure and other specialist staff to help develop activities for elderly people.

494 Sufficient account is not always taken of the recreational needs of elderly people in the planning, design and operation of indoor sports facilities.

495 Where there is a demand, time should be set aside at sports/leisure centres and swimming baths for elderly people to have exclusive use of some facilities at suitable times.

*__496__ Statutory authorities providing leisure facilities should consider the income of elderly people when fixing prices and wherever possible offer concessionary entry.

497 Local authorities should provide landscaped open spaces with adequate seating and within easy walking distance of residential areas.

498 Libraries are vital to the leisure of many elderly people. Consideration should be given to the shelving of books so that they are all accessible to elderly people. They should provide a wide selection of large print books, talking books and also records, cassettes and newspapers.

499 Small branch libraries should be maintained and the service of mobile libraries expanded to bring books and other facilities within easy reach of elderly people.

500 Co-operative schemes which enable elderly people to share their gardening skills and which could, at the same time, help them to maintain their gardens and allotments are welcome.

EUROPE

*501 The European Commission should examine the impact on elderly people of all proposed EEC policies and programmes.

*502 A forum should exist within Europe for organisations of retired people to express their views to the EEC.

*503 More comparative research should take place on the situation of elderly people in Europe.

*504 Retirement programmes and vocational training should be provided for workers over the age of 50 and money should be available for this purpose from the European Social Fund.

*505 Retirement ages for men and women should be the same throughout the EEC with necessary changes in income provision plus greater flexibility and choice on when to retire for Europe's workers.

*506 A card should exist for Europe's elderly people, giving a common entitlement to concessions throughout the EEC.

Memberships

Age Concern England's commitment to co-operation with a wide variety of organisations at local and national level can be seen from the list below of those which are members of its Governing Body, as from 31 March 1985.

Abbeyfield Society
Anchor Housing Association
Association of Charity Officers
Association of County Councils
Association of Directors of Social Services
Association of District Councils
Association of Metropolitan Authorities
Baptist Union of Great Britain and Ireland
British Association of Occupational Therapists
British Association of Social Workers
British Association of Settlements
British Geriatrics Society
British Medical Association
British Psychological Society
British Red Cross Society
British Refugee Council
British Society of Gerontology
Catholic Women's League and National Board
    of Catholic Women
Centre for Policy on Ageing
Chest Heart and Stroke Association
Church Army
Church of England Board of Social Responsibility
Civil Service Pensioners Alliance

Blind bowling club at King George's Park, Wandsworth.

Civil Service Retirement Fellowship
Community Projects Foundation
Confederation of British Industry
Counsel and Care for the Elderly
Disabled Living Foundation
Employment Fellowship
Family Welfare Association
Hanover Housing Association
Health Visitors Association
Help the Aged
Institute of Home Help Organisers
Institute of Health Service Administrators
Institute of Social Welfare
Jewish Welfare Board
Lions International
Methodist Homes for the Aged
National and Local Government Officers Association
National Association of Almshouses
National Association of Leagues of Hospital Friends
National Association of Mental Health
National Association of Town and Parish Councils
National Association of Women's Clubs
National Council for Carers and their Elderly Dependants
National Council for Voluntary Organisations
National Council of Women of Great Britain
National Federation of Community Organisations
National Federation of Housing Associations
National Federation of Post Office and British Telecom
    Pensioners
National Federation of Women's Institutes
National Free Church Women's Council
National Health Service Retirement Fellowship
National Institute of Adult Education
National Union of Teachers
Patients Association
Pre-Retirement Association
Queen's Medical Institute
Rotary International of Great Britain
Royal Association of Disability and Rehabilitation
Royal College of General Practitioners
Royal College of Nursing and NCN of the UK
Royal College of Psychiatrists Section for Psychiatry of Old Age
Royal National Institute for the Blind
Royal National Institute for the Deaf
Salvation Army
St John Ambulance Brigade
Social Care Association

Society of Friends
Society of Community Medicine
Soroptomist International of Great Britain and Ireland
Toc H Women's Association
Trades Union Congress
UK Federation of Business and Professional Women
Volunteer Centre
Women's Royal Voluntary Service

The Structure of Age Concern on pages 14–15 shows the relationship between the organisations listed above, the national centre of Age Concern and the various groups in the field.

Acknowledgements for photographs

Page 3   South Wales Evening Post
Page 30   Margaret Murray
Pages 48 and 90   Bob Roper
Pages 54, 110 and 124   Jewish Welfare Board
Pages 59 and 117   Tony Othen
Page 64   Shelter, Ferndale Project
Page 69   New Scotland Yard
Page 77   Sunil Gupta
Page 84   Anne Marie Stringfellow, Salisbury College of Art
Pages 95 and 107   British Telecom
Page 100   Newark Advertiser
Page 128   Wandsworth Photo Co-op

A selection of Age Concern England publications

Gardening in Retirement   £1.95

Isobel Pays describes how older people can get maximum enjoyment from plant growing in spite of minimum resources in the way of money, space or physical effort. There is information on light-weight garden tools, plus ideas for transforming a concrete patch, balcony or window sill. Experienced 'old time' gardeners will appreciate new and up to date tips while 'first timers' will welcome this easy to follow guide to a new and absorbing hobby.

In Touch with Cataracts   £1

Margaret Ford based the booklet on the many queries from elderly listeners to BBC Radio 4's 'In Touch' programme. Every year over 20,000 cataract operations are carried out mainly on elderly patients who often worry needlessly while waiting for their operation. There is pre-operative advice on coping with partial sight during the waiting period, an account of the operation and its after-effects.

A Home from Home   £4

This Research Unit report studies short-term family placement schemes for elderly people in Leeds, Liverpool and Leicestershire.

Management for Continence   £1.50

A much acclaimed book which suggests methods for the successful control of incontinence to improve the quality of life for elderly people and to save time for those caring for them. Author Bob Browne, a former geriatric nurse, draws on his own extensive experience in working with elderly people.

Staying Put: 55p
Help for Older Home Owners

Published in association with Anchor Housing Trust, the book explains the range of Government grants and financial help available. A list of Staying Put schemes is given with further sources of help and information.

Index